AUERBACH ON

DIGITAL PLOTTERS AND IMAGE DIGITIZERS

AUERBACH ON series

Published:

Optical Character Recognition
Alphanumeric Displays
Automatic Photocomposition
Microfilm Readers/Printers
Digital Plotters and Image Digitizers

Coming:

Computer Output Microfilm
Data Collection Systems
Data Communications
Programming Aids
Facsimile
Small Business Computers
Key to Storage
Compilers
Software

AUERBACH ON

DIGITAL PLOTTERS AND IMAGE DIGITIZERS

AUERBACH®
publishers

princeton
philadelphia
new york
london

Published simultaneously in Canada by Book Center, Inc.

Library of Congress Catalog Card Number: 70-189533
International Standard Book Number: 0-87769-123-1

First Printing

Printed in the United States of America

TABLE OF CONTENTS

PREFACE

This volume is one of a series of books covering significant developments in the information science industry. *AUERBACH on Digital Plotters and Image Digitizers* presents a comprehensive survey of plotting and digitizing devices in the current United States market and includes such aspects as suppliers, markets, applications, methods of use, and current technologies. Detailed technical descriptions are provided for the types of devices currently available. Characteristics of typical available devices appear in summary form in the comparison charts, included as Appendixes II and III.

Digital plotters and image digitizers are conveniently handled in a joint survey because of their close relationship. The action of a digital plotter in providing graphical computer output is complemented by that of an image digitizer, which generates a digitally coded representation of graphic information used as input. Frequently, the devices function together in the same system; graphic input to a computer system by a digitizer can be redrawn on a digital plotter after computer processing. These combined systems result in a certain overlap between the device types in market and application, particularly in the area of automatic drafting systems; however, neither plotters nor digitizers are confined to these joint application areas. Another common feature of digital plotters and image digitizers is diversification into a wide variety of functions, applications, and costs, which reflects an imaginative willingness of suppliers to exploit new or unconventional technologies in the attempt to capture untapped markets.

AUERBACH on Digital Plotters and Image Digitizers is an expansion of material that originated in *AUERBACH Computer Technology Reports,* a series of loose-leaf services recognized as the standard guide to EDP throughout the world. The reports are prepared and edited by the publisher's staff of professional EDP specialists.

Material in this volume was current at the time of preparation; however, the field is changing so rapidly that the publishers cannot guarantee completeness of the contents. To get the most recent information on equipment and the significant companies that produce it, refer to *AUERBACH Computer Technology Reports*. Information can be obtained from the publisher, AUERBACH Publishers, Inc., 121 North Broad Street, Philadelphia, Pa. 19107.

AUERBACH ON

DIGITAL PLOTTERS AND IMAGE DIGITIZERS

1. GENERAL INTRODUCTION

A broad class of computer applications concerns the manipulation of graphical information, which must be handled in digital form within the computer. Computer graphics applications range from the simple computer output of a graph that displays a mathematical function or a business trend, to sophisticated applications involving the computer generation or modification of such extensive graphics as engineering drawings, electronic circuit artwork, maps, and clothing patterns.

One important application area involves the preparation of control tapes for numerically controlled machine tools; use of computer graphics here includes generation of tapes for the machining of parts specified by drawings input to the computer and the production of verification plots for numerical control tapes prior to testing on the machine tools themselves. Many other application areas will be mentioned in subsequent chapters.

Computer manipulation of graphical data is primarily served by the devices discussed in this book. Digital plotters move a plotting tool or a beam of light over a plotting surface in two dimensions under digital control, while image digitizers perform the inverse function of generating a digital representation to the shape of a curve followed by some kind of sensor. Computer-driven devices involving the display of information directly on a cathode-ray tube or on microfilm are excluded from this publication, since their technologies, applications, and markets are sufficiently different to warrant separate treatments.

Though digital plotters and image digitizers are used jointly in many applications, particularly those involving automatic drafting, the overlap in market and application areas is only partial—both plotter and digitizer groups include models with a wide range of applications and corresponding diversification in function, technology, and price. Plotters and digitizers are therefore treated separately herein, with areas common to both indicated as they occur.

The rest of this book consists of separate but parallel parts on digital plotters and image digitizers, and the appendixes provide comparison chart and manufacturer directory sections. Each major part starts with an introductory chapter, which gives a general overview of the types of devices available and their applications, suppliers, and markets. The introductory chapter also classifies the available equipment, to create a basis for the discussions in subsequent chapters. These chapters include detailed technical discussions of the construction and operation of representative available devices—that is, of machines that are good examples of their specific types. The devices chosen are those whose description best clarifies the applications and operating principle of each category; no implication that they are the top models or most successful of their kind is intended.

Appendixes to the book include comparison charts, which give outline technical specifications of currently available plotters and digitizers; a manufacturer directory is also included. Comparison charts permit quick evaluation, but they give little insight to construction and operating principles. A more intelligent use of comparison charts and other simplified summaries can be made if the basic nature of the different kinds of plotters and digitizers is understood. Hence, comparison charts are most meaningful when used in conjunction with the contents of the entire book, with reference to the tutorial introductions to plotters and digitizers and the more detailed chapters on particular device categories.

PART I—DIGITAL PLOTTERS

2. INTRODUCTION TO DIGITAL PLOTTERS

BACKGROUND AND DEVELOPMENT

Automatic digital plotters—which produce hard-copy graphic output from computer-generated digital data—have been developed for an amazingly wide range of applications. From small beginnings as output devices for graphical presentation of the results of scientific and mathematical calculations, their province has spread to cover such diverse applications as management information, automatic drafting, preparation of printed-circuit artwork, verification of input programs prepared for numerically controlled machine tools, and cloth cutting for tailoring. This chapter introduces the potential use of automatic digital plotters in data processing installations by describing the development of such devices, the different types of plotters available, and the ways in which the latter operate and are put to use.

The success of digital plotters in a large number of highly diversified applications has led to the introduction of a correspondingly large range of new devices as the various marketing areas are exploited. Low-cost digital plotters, selling for about $3000, include models that interface to a data communications line and can be used to produce 11x17-inch plots of scientific data from time-sharing systems. At the other end of the scale are enormous automatic drafting systems, which can produce precision working drawings up to 6x24 feet and sell for nearly a quarter of a million dollars per unit. An important specialized market within this group is the area of printed-circuit artwork preparation, for which extremely precise, photo-

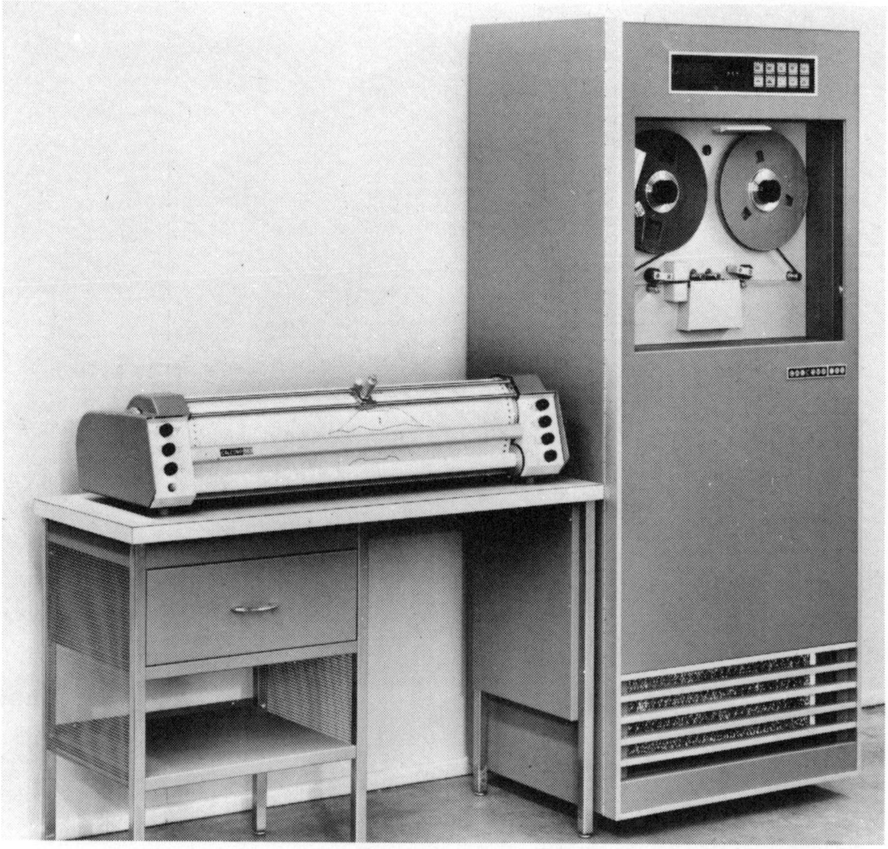

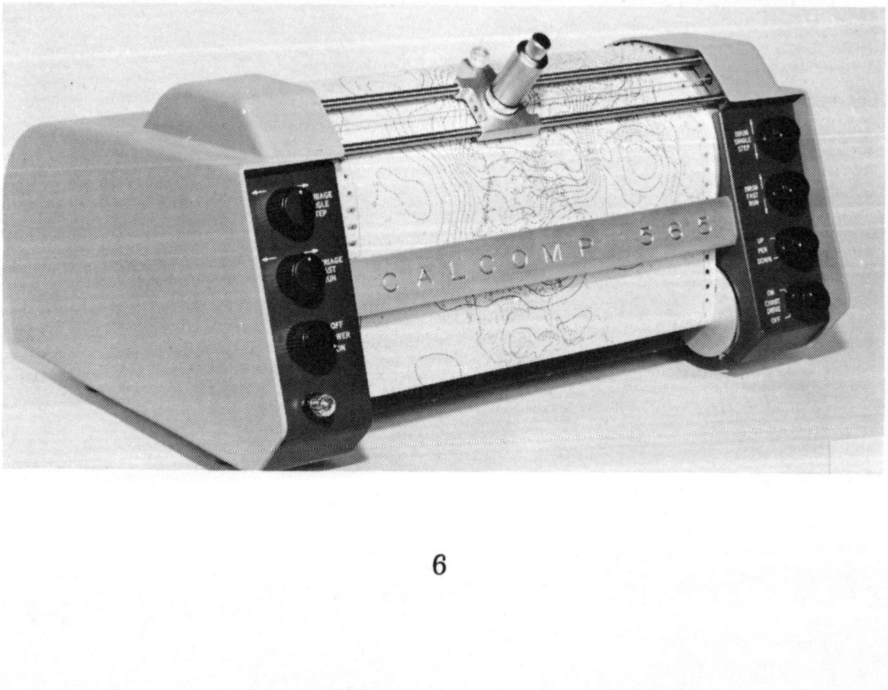
CALCOMP 565

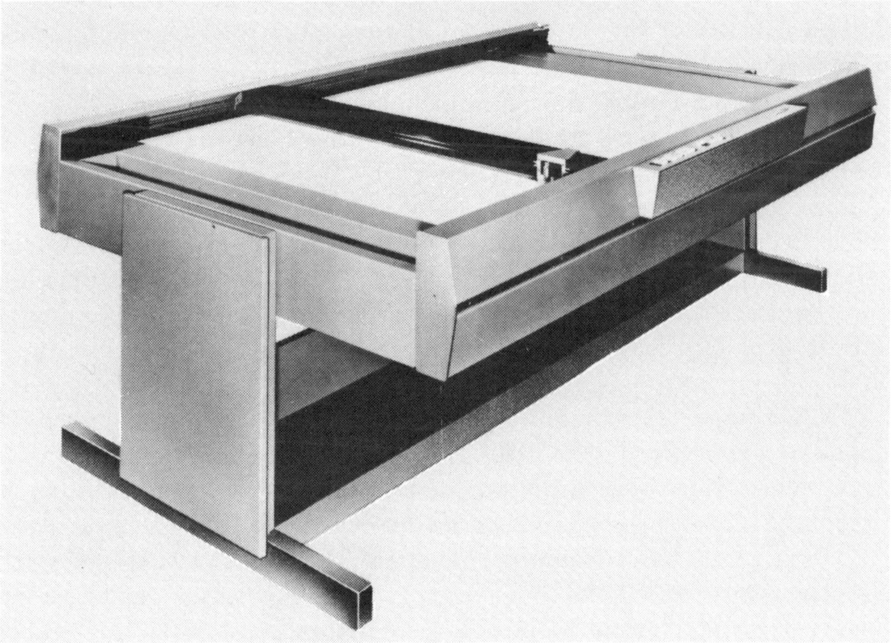

Fig. 2-1. CalComp digital plotters.

graphic plotting is required; a number of specially developed digital plotters are now available for this purpose.

This chapter, and the more detailed chapters that follow it, cover the full variety of digital plotters from the very small to the very large. However, digital recorders in which a clock controls paper motion beneath recording styli are not considered; nor are nonimpact printers, graphic displays, and computer output microfilmers with graphical capabilities. Eliminating these types of units confines us to devices that move a pen, a stylus, or a beam of light in two directions over a plotting surface under digital control. Crude digital plots are sometimes obtained from teleprinters and line printers, but these are not considered here.

Some representative digital plotters are shown in Figure 2-1. The initial types developed were analog plotters, which accepted analog input signals to control pen movement and were generally associated with analog devices. Most continuous strip recorders are of this kind. If an analog plotter is to be connected to a digital computer, a special digital-to-analog interface is required to convert the digital outputs of the computer to the analog signals required by the plotter.

The first plotter to accept analog input was developed by Electronics Associates, Inc., in 1946; and digital-to-analog converters, which allowed these devices to accept information from digital computers, first appeared in the early 1950s. These early point-plotters were used mainly for data reduction and wind-tunnel analysis. They could only plot points and were slow, crude, and unreliable by current standards.

Digital plotters were developed later for direct connection with digital computers. These not only eliminated the need for special digital-to-analog converters but also allowed use of the more precise controls inherent in digital operations. Digital plotters can be used in more general applications than can their analog counterparts, just as digital computers are more flexible than analog systems. Digital plotters eliminate the problems of drift, dynamic response, and changing gain settings that are inherent in analog operations.

Plotter improvements followed the more extensive development of digital computers during the 1950s. Line-drawing capabilities, for example, were pioneered by Benson-Lehner (now the Graphic Systems Division of Computer Industries) and Electronics Associates, Inc., in the mid-1950s. At the end of the 1950s, California Computer Products (CalComp) devised a plotter that used incremental stepping motors instead of analog servomotors. This new concept included a drum that passed sprocket-hole paper back and forth under a moving pen mounted on a fixed arm.

Other advances included the introduction of a range of automatic drafting machines by the Gerber Scientific Instrument Company, which offers flatbed plotting over areas up to 8x24 feet, and the development of spe-

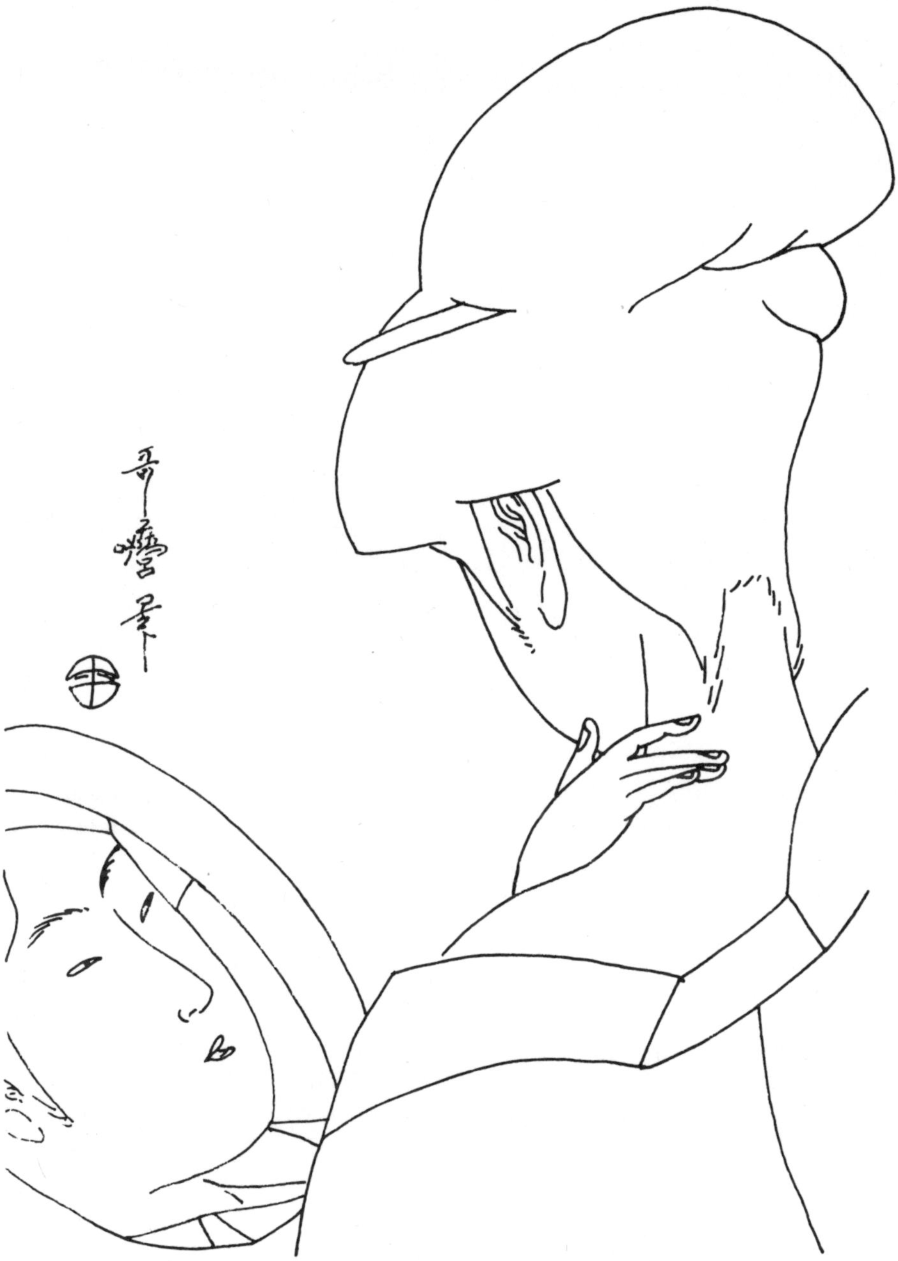

Fig. 2-2. CalComp plotter reproduction of an eighteenth century Japanese woodblock print.

cialized plotting systems for the production of electronic artwork. (See Figs. 2-2 and 2-3 for examples of plotter output.) Some digital plotters have pioneered new plotting technologies: for example, the Dresser Systems LGP 2000, which uses a spot of laser light to develop a plot by suc-

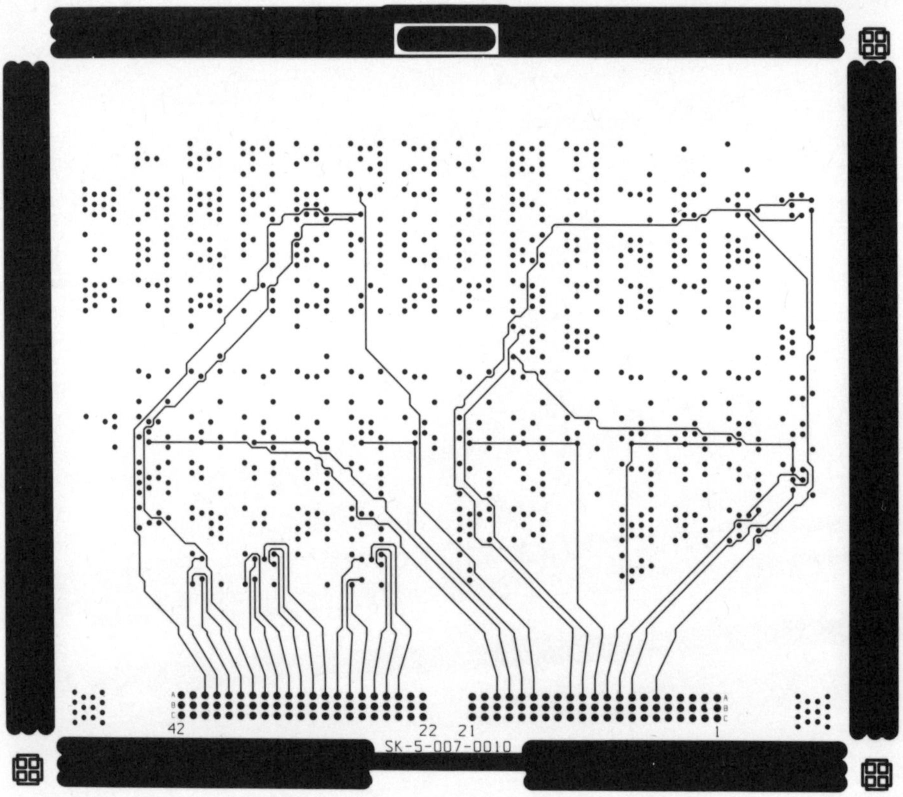

Fig. 2-3. Example of a backboard-circuit layout produced by a Gerber scientific plotter.

cessive scans of a photographic film; and the plotters introduced by Xynetics, Inc., which use linear induction motors to control the movement of a freely running plotting head over the plotting surface.

An important contribution to the widespread use of digital plotters is due to the development of digital plotter software. Programming for the use of digital plotters is tedious and costly, so the advent of software for standard plotter operations has added enormously to the general popularity of digital plotting. CalComp remains an industry leader in the supply of plotter software; a discussion of the CalComp software is included in Chapter 3.

APPLICATION AREAS

The development of digital plotters is still a very active field, as more applications and new plotting technologies are explored. Further developments can be expected as the use of digital plotters increases. Especially significant for general-purpose computer installations is the expansion of application areas that digital plotters can provide (noted later). EDP managers, operations research staffs, marketing functions, and manufacturing processes can benefit equally from the addition of a digital plotting capability to a general-purpose computer.

In the last decade, digital plotters have made exceptional strides in both performance and scope of application. The resolution, accuracy, and repeatability of present flatbed plotters, for instance, have sharply reduced the role of the draftsman in many large industries such as airframe, automobile, engine, machine tool, and heavy electrical and hydraulic equipment manufacturing, to mention only a partial list.

The monitoring of scientific and medical processes by drum plotters is also growing steadily. A significant application of comparatively recent origin is the creation of patterns from which the masks used in fabricating semiconductor chips are reproduced. Similarly, patterns utilized in the numerical control of automated manufacturing processes are both tentatively confirmed and eventually executed for use by appropriate plotters. Rubylith cutting heads are especially valuable in this field. Plotters with suitable cutting heads have even been devised to cut cloth patterns for the clothing industry. Neither should the extensive role of digital plotters in architecture be overlooked.

In contrast, the advancement of plotters into commercial activities, management information systems, operations research functions, and general data processing has been severely inhibited by difficulties in competing with alternative methods. The basic limitation is insufficient volume to compensate for substantial costs arising from several sources. These costs include capital expenditures for the plotting system—such as interfaces and accessories, or the leasing charges for a rented system—fees for application software, programming costs, and labor charges prorated according to execution time.

It is interesting to note that in these fields the chief competitor of the digital plotter is the draftsman, who is not ready to become extinct just yet. When a decision for automatic plotting in EDP applications is made, a first cousin of the digital plotter—the nonimpact printer-plotter—is usually given preference because of its ability to print and thus support the impact printer serving as the primary output device.

Another related device, the computer output microfilmer, is gradually gaining ground in environments calling for numerous duplicate copies, or mass distribution, or the storage and rapid retrieval of many document pages, or any combination of these requirements. Another competitor is the display terminal, both alphanumeric and graphic, especially when combined with a hard-copy printer. The electronic plotter—actually a noninteractive form of the graphic display terminal that provides a hard-copy printout within moments after the visual display has been executed—finds occasional service in this area as well. For the digital plotter to vie successfully with its alternatives in the foregoing applications, a prerequisite is that the volume of plots required of it rise sufficiently to lower the cost per plot and the required duplicates, which must be produced in some suitable manner, to competitive levels.

We conclude that certain constraints are impeding the entry of the digital plotter into unaccustomed fields. For the present it will consolidate its preeminence in the following major categories: (1) the execution of high-resolution drawings in industry and architecture, all the more when these drawings are physically large or on a nonpaper medium like film or vellum; (2) continuous real-time translation of graphic data into eye-readable form in scientific and industrial processes; (3) scientific or geological plotting, such as weather maps, satellite and conventional cartography, geological charts, vapor chamber patterns, electric field gradient plots, and wind-tunnel patterns; (4) pattern plotting for printed circuits; (5) pattern plotting for semiconductor fabrication; and (6) pattern plotting and cutting for various numerical control applications.

CLASSIFICATION

Digital plotters are classified by type of plotting surface, recording technique, method of line drawing, or the manner of specifying the plot. From the standpoint of both operational mechanism and approximate division into market and applications areas, perhaps the most useful classification is by the method used to mount the plotting surface on the plotter. The two usual categories for this classification are drum-type plotters (in which the plot is produced by a combination of the motion of the plotting head from side to side and the motion of the plotting surface backward and forward) and flatbed plotters (in which the plotting head moves along two dimensions over a fixed plotting surface). This broad classification is useful, but it must be applied carefully to such borderline cases as the Houston Instrument plotters (which are clearly drum-type but have no drum, paper being passed between two fanfold piles instead) and the Gerber System 40, which is a special-purpose plotter for printed-circuit artwork generation and which has a large and elaborate photographic plotting head that remains stationary over a comparatively small (30x30 inches) plotting area (the plotting table moves below the head to produce the plot).

Besides the drum-type and flatbed plotters, there are a number of plotters operating with still other technologies. These are covered separately later, although they have features in common with both drum-type and flatbed plotters.

The classification framework presented here provides for the more detailed treatment of digital plotters in subsequent chapters: After a discussion in Chapter 3 of CalComp plotters (an important range of products touching on all of the most important classes of plotters), Chapter 4 deals with drum-type plotters, while flatbed plotters are the subject of Chapter 5, and other plotting technologies are discussed in Chapter 6. The following paragraphs introduce these different equipment classes briefly, concentrating on the variations between them.

Drum-Type Plotters

Drum-type plotters feature a movable plotting surface in conjunction with a writing carriage to provide the required two-dimensional motion. (Examples of drum-type plotters are the CalComp Models 563 and 565 shown in Figure 2-1.) In these units the writing element moves along one axis while rotation of the drum supplies movement along the other coordinate. At the present time, California Computer Products (CalComp), University Computing (UCC) and Houston Instrument, Division of Bausch and Lomb, are major manufacturers of drum plotters. Most of their units employ an incremental plotting technique that produces a graph by a series of fixed incremental steps of the drum and/or carriage. Bidirectional motors are used to control motion along both the X- and Y-axes so that each input digital signal causes a small incremental step (1/100 inch or less) of the carriage or the drum, or both. A third (Z-axis) input signal is used to control the raising and lowering of the pen from the surface of the paper.

Compared with table-type plotters, most drum-type plotters are compact, cost less, and capable of producing single plots as long as the roll of paper. The main disadvantages are that they can only produce plots on paper with a single tool, since paper is the only medium that can be fanfolded or rolled suitably and the plotting head assembly will support only a single plotting tool. Grid or preprinted forms can be used only if they are available in the correct rolled or fanfolded form; moreover, they are difficult to register, since it is difficult for the operator to see the plotting tool. For applications involving large amounts of plotting on paper, and where accuracy is not paramount, drum-type plotters offer an attractive solution to equipment requirements.

While most drum-type plotters are small, inexpensive units, other larger drum plotters have been developed for applications requiring fast and accurate plotting on paper. These devices, examples of which are those manufactured by CalComp, UCC, and Gerber Scientific, offer high plotting speeds combined with accuracies that compare favorably with those of many flatbed plotters. These models have found an important market in the verification plotting of electronics artwork data prior to the generation of the artwork on a flatbed plotter.

Flatbed Plotters

Flatbed, or table-type, plotters incorporate a flat plotting surface ranging in size from 11x17 inches to 6x24 feet. (Examples of flatbed plotters are the CalComp Models 502 and 718 shown in Figure 2-1.) The paper generally remains stationary throughout the plotting of a single graphic image; the plotting mechanism performs all necessary movements. (Automatic

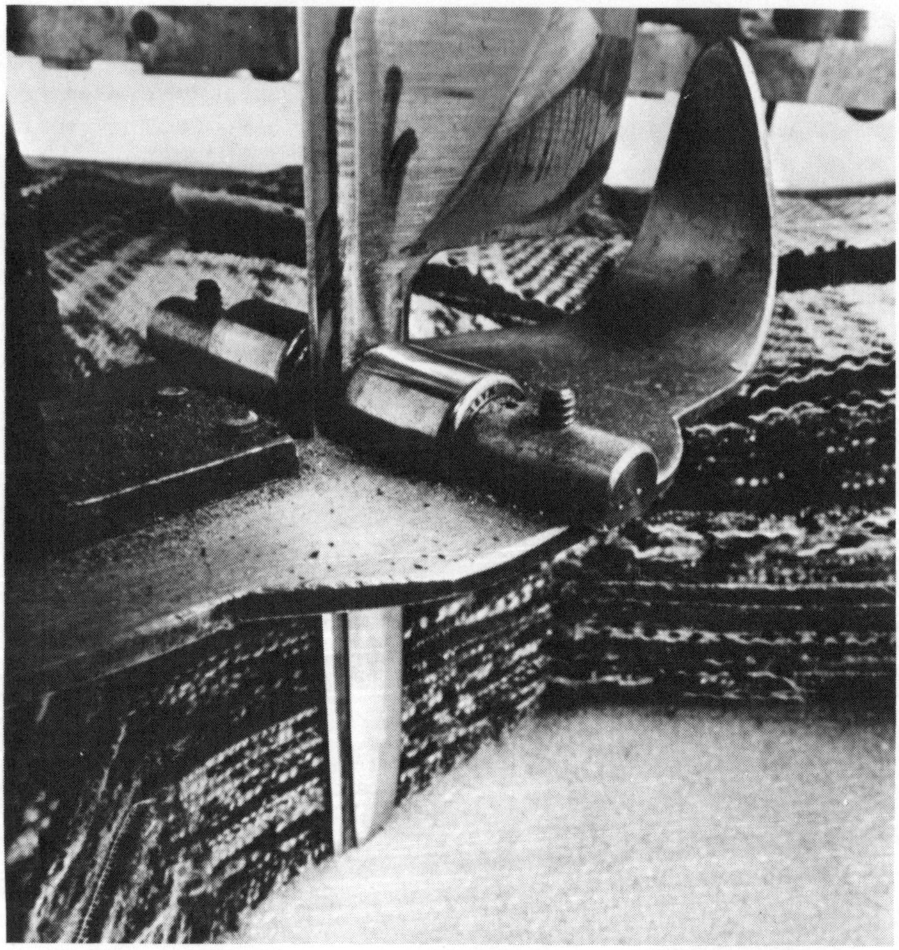

Fig. 2-4. Cloth-cutting head used with a Gerber plotting table.

paper feed is available optionally for many flatbed plotters, but is used only between one graphic image and the next.) The paper or some other plotting medium is usually held to the plotter surface by a vacuum applied from below. Generally, the plotters are operated with the plotting surface horizontal, although some models have a tiltable surface and can operate with the surface in any position from horizontal to vertical.

The writing mechanism consists of a carriage and writing-tool assembly that moves along one axis of the plotting surface; the tool assembly is also free to move along the other axis. Motion in the X- or Y-direction, or in both directions simultaneously, is thus obtained, enabling the plotting tool to reach any coordinate value within the plotting area. The tool can be raised for positioning. The positioning mechanism for table-type plotters usually consists of screw drives in the X- and Y-directions, which may be actuated by digital or analog signals. An altogether different type of analog positioning is used in the plotters produced by Xynetics Corporation; these are discussed under other plotting technologies.

Flatbed plotters in general are more versatile, accurate, and expensive than drum-type plotters. Because the plotting head is mounted on a large moving assembly, such options as multiple-tool heads or photographic plotting attachments are often among those offered. (See Fig. 2-4.) The special-purpose attachments available for table-type plotters frequently add to the control problems for the plotter as well as to its versatility—photographic plotting, for example, usually requires program selection of the aperture used. Special control electronics within the plotter hardware is sometimes needed for the use of these special tools. For instance, the speed of a variable-aperture photographic plotting head is automatically varied with the aperture selected and thus gives a constant film exposure; also, a cutting knife on the plotting head must be turned so that it always points in the current direction of motion.

Other Plotting Technologies

A number of plotters have been developed which use unconventional plotting technologies of great interest. A case in point is the flatbed plotter manufactured by Xynetics, Inc. (Fig. 2-5), which uses the proprietary "Sawyer principle" drive for the plotting head. In these devices, a cushion of compressed air supports the free-running plotting head. Analog positioning signals pass to electromagnets in the head, which interact with a fixed waffle-iron pattern of magnetic material beneath the plotting surface to produce plotting movement on the principle of a linear induction motor. The Xynetics plotters can attain remarkable plotting speeds because of the low inertia of the plotting head.

Film plotters, which produce output on photographic film, are not

Fig. 2-5. Xynetics 1100 automatic drafting system.

strictly a separate device class, since optical plotting heads are available for many flatbed plotters.

Flatbed film plotting is generally used for printed-circuit artwork applications, an area already noted. Film plotting is unavailable for drum-type plotters, since photographic plotting heads have not been developed for this type of equipment.

Besides the flatbed plotters and some microfilm plotters, which are outside the scope of the present discussion, there are certain specialized plotters designed exclusively for photographic plotting. One example is the digital plotting system manufactured by GeoSpace Corporation, which uses a cathode-ray tube projection technique to generate an image on photographic film. Another approach, used by Dresser Systems in their LGP 2000, is to generate an image directly on film by left-to-right scans of a laser beam deflected by a mirror. Advantages of the laser plotting technique are that plots in different shades of gray can be produced by modulating the beam, and plots as long as a roll of film (100 feet) can be produced; the facility for long plots is particularly important for the seismic applications for which the LGP 2000 was originally developed.

PLOTTING PROCESS

Most drum-type and flatbed plotters operate in an incremental mode in which the plotting tool moves across the plotting medium in a rapid succession of small steps. The direction of each step is selected by the input

Plotter Movement

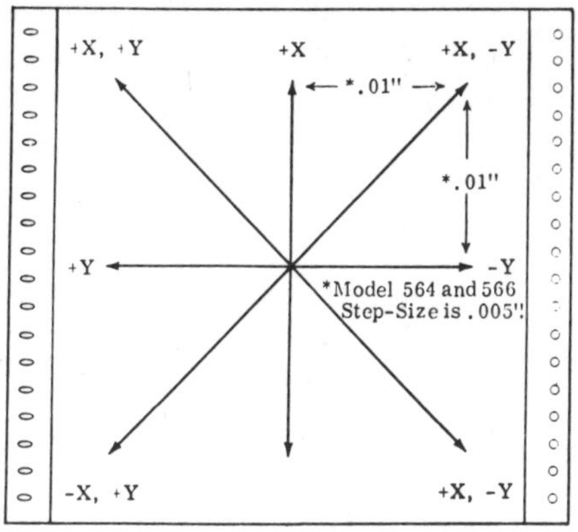

Instruction Characters

1130 Character	0	1	2	3	4	5	6	7	8	9
Plotter Operation	Pen Down	+Y	+Y, +X	+X	-Y, +X	-Y	-Y, -X	-X	+Y, -X	Pen Up

Fig. 2-6. Control characters for plot operation.

data from one of eight (less frequently, 16 or 24) directions. Figure 2-6 shows the pen directions corresponding to each of the permissible input characters for a CalComp drum plotter operated on-line to an IBM 1130 computer, an arrangement typical of many plotting systems.

Since only a few line directions are available, lines and curves generated by an incremental plotter tend to have a stepped appearance. The jaggedness can be reduced by using a plotter with shorter step lengths (some plotters offer a selection of step lengths), but this tends to slow down operation because the plotting head must generally come to rest at the end of each step. Because of their constant stopping and starting, incremental plotters are generally noisy while operating.

Digital stepper motors are generally used in incremental plotters, although a combination of analog and digital techniques is sometimes used. Some equipment has features to alleviate the disadvantages of the stepwise operation of incremental plotters. For instance, CalComp offers facilities for drawing lines at any angle in a single operation. Other systems (e.g., Gerber Scientific Instrument Company) have a velocity-control feature so that the plotting head, instead of coming to rest after each step, is simply accelerated and decelerated sufficiently to negotiate changes in direction in the line being plotted.

An alternative method is to use analog signals for the positioning of the plotting head; this has the advantage of eliminating stepwise operation.

In analog systems, digital input commands are converted to analog levels by a digital-to-analog converter. A feedback device monitors the movement of the servomotor, and an error-detection signal is generated to drive the plotting head to the required position. Early servomotor drive systems were subject to drift, and accuracy was dependent on voltage stability; this is currently the case with some low-cost analog positioning systems. Several manufacturers use hybrid positioning, which includes features of both analog and digital methods. One example of such a device is the EAI 430 DATAPLOTTER®.*

Plotting System Considerations

In nearly all digital plotter applications, the plot data is generated or processed by a digital computer, although in some cases the data is generated by image digitizers, coordinate digitizers, or digital recording instruments. In any case, the plotter is not used in isolation but serves as one component of a system that produces the final plot.

Remote graphic output is a new application for digital plotters. A typical example of this is the California Computer Products Model 210 remote plotter controller. This device permits connection of any CalComp 500 or 600 Series plotter and a separate teleprinter to a communications line. With this configuration, a computer system can service a large number of plotter terminals at transmission speeds up to 300 bits per second; and remote terminals can interrogate the computer system for graphic information.

Digital plotters frequently connect on-line (i.e., by direct, local connection) to a digital computer. In on-line use, the plotter operates the same way as any other computer peripheral, responding to commands and data relayed from the computer program. Control exerted by the computer in such cases is usually straightforward; an incremental plotter on line to a computer, for example, responds to a sequence of step specifications received across the computer interface.

While on-line plotting is adequate for small-scale scientific plotting, it is somewhat unsatisfactory in general because many plotters operate rather slowly by computer standards. The alternative is off-line working, in which computer-generated data (usually on magnetic tape, but alternatively on punched cards or paper tape) is plotted after its generation by the computer, releasing the main computer for other tasks while plotting takes place.

Off-line plotting requires more sophisticated control than on-line plot-

*The name DATAPLOTTER® is a registered trademark of Electronic Associates, Inc.

ting because the operation of the plotter must be coordinated with that of the peripheral device from which the data for the plot is taken. Some plotters can connect directly to a computer peripheral for off-line working, but in those cases the handling of the peripheral is rudimentary. For instance, plot data may be read one character at a time from magnetic tape, using an incremental magnetic-tape reader. More sophisticated off-line plotting systems require the use of a *plotter controller* to coordinate the actions of the plotter and the data input device.

Plotter controllers range in sophistication from simple device interconnectors to elaborate pieces of equipment incorporating minicomputers. An example of one elementary function that might be performed by a plotter controller would be the buffered reading of the input peripheral device, which allows data to be read from the device simultaneously with plotter operation. More elaborate controllers perform such functions as reading the data for a number of steps ahead of the current plotting position and performing an analysis of the curve being drawn, to optimize the velocity of the plotting head; in such a case, throughput is increased, since the plotting head need not halt after each step, although this is at the expense of considerable elaboration in the controller.

Some of the more elaborate controllers also process the input data so that it can be more economically represented. For example, a line to be drawn on an incremental plotter might be specified by a controller command followed by the coordinates of its end points, leaving the controller to generate the series of steps necessary to draw the line. This particular capability, known as linear interpolation, is particularly valuable when test plots are to be produced from input tapes for numerically controlled machine tools, because such interpolation is one of the standard functions of these tools. (Control tapes for machine tools are usually prepared in accordance with standards of the Electronics Industries Association; therefore plotter controllers that also conform to these standards are attractive for machine-tool tape verification; circular as well as linear interpolation is included in the EIA standards.)

The available range of plotter controllers is exemplified by units offered by the Gerber Scientific Instrument Company for their automatic drafting systems. In order of increasing complexity, these controllers and their functions are—

1. Series 500 controller: a hardwired, linear interpolator for on-line use of the plotting tables.
2. Series 600 controller: a hardwired, linear interpolator with off-line plotting, using data taken from paper-tape reader, keyboard, or buffered magnetic-tape reader.

3. Series 400 and 700 controllers: programmed controllers for off-line use, offering buffered input and linear and circular interpolation.

4. Series 1200 controller: a more elaborate version of the Series 700 controller, also offering some data look-ahead and optional digitizing capabilities. (See Fig. 2-7.)

5. Series 2000 controller: a more sophisticated version of the Series 1200 controller, including parabolic interpolation and full data look-ahead with consequent optimization of the velocity of the plotting head.

Fig. 2-7. Gerber Series 1200 controller, Model 75, large-area drafting table and Teletypewriter.

SOFTWARE

The exact form of the data needed to operate a digital plotter depends on the type of plotter in use. An incremental plotter, for example, requires a series of characters, each specifying one step in the movement of the plotting head over the plotting medium and interspersed with commands to control the plotting head. Not only is the data format dependent on the particular plotter in use, but it is also arranged very awkwardly from the point of view of a computer programmer who wishes to generate a particular plot that may involve, for example, the specification and annotation of axes and the generation of line segments and curves of different types for the graphics being generated.

In practice, these restrictions make plotter programming so time consuming that it is impractical in the absence of special plotter routines—that is, software supplied so that the plotter accepts data in a form more relevant to programming of computer graphics applications than the data

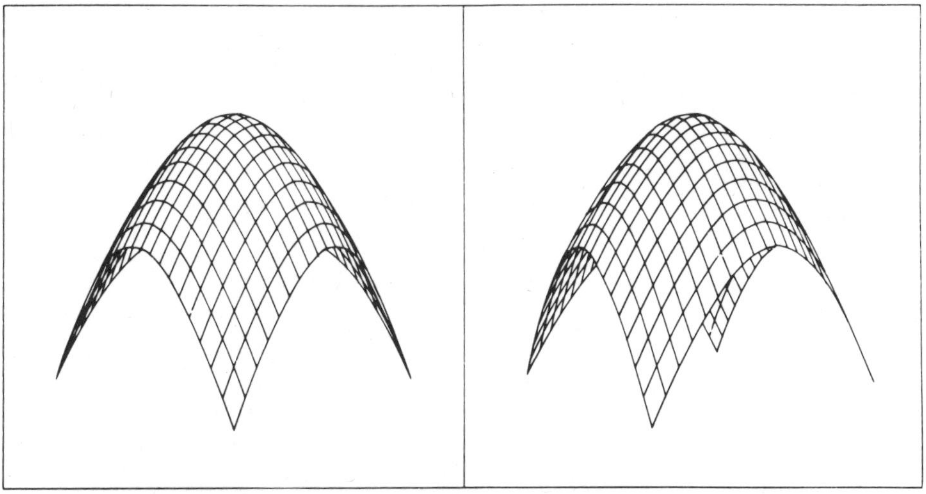

Fig. 2-8. Examples of perspective plots of three-dimensional surfaces produced with standard digital plotter software packages.

formats that the plotter itself requires. This plotting software may take the form of routines for standard operations such as the drawing of line segments or characters and axes; in this case the routines are usually arranged as a package usable by a programmer working in FORTRAN or some other high-level programming language; alternatively, complete plotting programs may be supplied for particular applications such as the drawing of PERT charts, engineering plans, or perspective plots of three-dimensional surfaces. (See Fig. 2-8.) Plotter software of this type is generally supplied by the plotter manufacturer. In addition to this software, the manufacturer may also be expected to furnish comprehensive programming when a complete system is offered for some application like electronic artwork preparation or when a controller is provided for the plotter that incorporates a minicomputer.

The writer of a computer program to produce graphical output is particularly interested in knowing details of the plotter subroutines provided by the manufacturer, and in this area there is considerable variation. Some manufacturers simply provide basic routines for the output of lines and circular arcs; others have more elaborate routines covering such facilities as output of characters, specification of axes for graphical plots, drawing of contour maps, and generation of perspective views of three-dimensional surfaces. In general, the writing of computer programs to produce graphical output represents considerable investments in time and money, so the software complement should be evaluated carefully whenever a plotter is selected.

3. CALCOMP PRODUCTS, A REPRESENTATIVE RANGE OF DIGITAL PLOTTERS

INTRODUCTION AND OVERVIEW

Because of the great range of digital plotters available—which includes widely different device types, costs, and applications—it is not surprising to find that the market for digital plotters is divided into a number of submarkets, each with its own principal suppliers and characteristic customers. Examples of suppliers specializing largely in one market segment are UCC and Houston Instrument for drum-type plotters; Hewlett-Packard for time-sharing plotting systems; and Universal Drafting, Gerber Scientific, Tridea, and Kongsberg for large flatbed plotting systems and automatic drafting machines. Several of these manufacturers and their products are discussed further in subsequent chapters.

The only plotter manufacturer that has successfully penetrated all of the market areas mentioned is California Computer Products (CalComp); CalComp, the undisputed leader in many market segments, has developed an integrated product line of drum and flatbed plotters which embraces every specialization noted. Because of CalComp's commanding position within the digital plotter industry, its product line serves both as an illustration of most of the topics in Chapter 2 and in other areas (for instance, in the provision of software) as an example that other suppliers are anxious to emulate. Thus, a comprehensive discussion of the CalComp digital plotters is a useful introduction to the more restricted discussions of the succeeding chapters.

California Computer Products, the pioneer and leading supplier of

Table 3-1. Characteristics of CalComp Digital Plotters

CHARACTERISTICS	SERIES 500			SERIES 600		SERIES 700		1136 DRUM PLOTTER
General								
Max operating speed, steps/sec	300			700; 900		700; 900 (ZIP mode equivalent to 1687)		2600
Max axial plotting speeds, ips	3.0			Up to 4.5, depending on model & step size		Up to 16.87		6.5
No. of vectors	8			24		24		24
ZIP® Mode*	No			No		Yes		No
Notes	(1)			(2)		—		(3)
Drum Plotter Model	*563*	*565*	*575*	*663*	*665*	*763*	*765*	*1136*
Plot width, inches	29.5	11	11	29.5	11	29.5	11	12; 34
Step size, inches	0.010/0.005/0.1 mm			0.010/0.005; 0.005/0.0025; 0.0025/0.00125				0.0025
Flatbed Plotter Model	*502*			*602*	*638*	*702*	*738*	*745*
Plot size, inches	31X34			31X34	48X72	31X34	48X72	48X60
Step size, inches	0.010, 0.005, 0.002			0.005/0.0025	0.002/0.001	0.005/0.025; 0.002/0.001	0.001/0.002; 0.002/0.004; 0.001/0.0005	0.0001
Step size, mm	0.1/0.05			0.1/0.15	0.05/0.025	0.1/0.05; 0.05/0.025;	0.05/0.025 0.025/0.0125	

*ZIP® is a registered trademark of California Computer Products, Inc.

Notes:

(1) 575 has data communications interface for remote plotting.
(2) Accepts 500 Series or 700 Series input data; two switch-selectable step sizes per model.
(3) Two interchangeable drums of different widths.

low-cost drum-plotter systems for on-line computer use, has enlarged its line of digital plotting systems to cover an extensive number of markets. Current CalComp digital plotting systems include both drum and flatbed plotters, with a range of controls, interfaces, and accessories for on-line, remote (time sharing), and off-line plotting applications. Recent additions include high-precision flatbed plotters and systems for electronics artwork applications.

From its initial drum plotter products, the company has diversified as well as enlarged its line of digital plotting systems; other CalComp products include microfilm plotters, industry-compatible disk storage units, and data entry systems.

Although CalComp digital plotting systems vary in capabilities, cost, and applications, they share common operating concepts and interfaces, and so all of their systems are covered herein. There are two major components: the plotters (both drum and flatbed) and their controls (interfaces for direct connection to local or remote computers or to systems for off-line digital plotting).

Characteristics of the CalComp digital plotters are summarized in Table 3-1. (Four of these plotters appear in Fig. 2-1.) The 14 different plotters are grouped into four classes: 500 Series, 600 Series, 700 Series, and the Model 1136 drum plotter. Plotters in the same series have similar operating characteristics. The 500, 600, and 700 Series are arranged in order of increasing cost and performance, while the Model 1136 drum

Table 3-2. Plotter Controllers and Interfaces for On-Line Use of Plotters

110 SERIES CONTROLLERS		INTERFACES AND INTERFACE KITS	
MODEL NO.	HOST COMPUTER	MODEL NO.	HOST COMPUTER
110	IBM/360 Model 30, 40, or 50	J516	Honeywell DDP-516, H316
111	CDC 3000 Series	J1130	IBM 1130 on-line interface
112	G-400 and G-600 Series		
113	RCA Spectra 70 Series	J1130A	IBM 1130 on-line interface for two plotters
114	XDS 925/930/940/9400		
115	Univac 9000 Series		
116	XDS Sigma Series	J1130B	IBM 1130 on-line interface*
117	IBM 1800		
118	Univac Defense and Commercial Computers	J1401	IBM 1401
119	NCR Century Series		
120	Phillips P1000 Series	J1620	IBM 1620

*For 1136 or 745 plotters only.

plotter is noted for its speed. The latest of the CalComp plotting tables, Model 745, is a high-precision flatbed plotter with a granite plotting surface.

The controls and interfaces available for CalComp plotters reflect different operating configurations. Those for direct on-line computer use are listed in Table 3-2; besides those shown, standard interfaces for the use of CalComp 500 Series digital plotters are offered by a number of computer manufacturers. Remote operation of CalComp plotters is provided by the use of the Series 200 or Series 600 remote plotter interfaces, as listed in Table 3-3; the 575 drum plotter, however, can be connected directly to a data communication link for remote plotting. Off-line digital plotting is controlled by a CalComp plotter in conjunction with either one of the magnetic-tape units detailed in Table 3-4 or the Model 900 controller, a free-standing, programmable controller that provides more sophisticated plotter control than any of the magnetic-tape units; the Model 900 control must be used in combination with the Model 937 magnetic-tape unit. Models 900 and 937 must be used in order to gain the full operating potential of the Series 700 plotters; they can also be used with the CalComp 800 and 1600 Series microfilm plotters, which are outside the scope of this report. A CalComp digital plotting system that comprises a controller and a plotter is identified by double model numbers; for example, the Model 900 controller and Model 937 magnetic-tape unit combined with the 1136 drum plotter make up the 900/937/1136 digital plotting system.

Table 3-3. CalComp Remote Plotter Interfaces

MODEL NO.	DESCRIPTION	FUNCTION
200 Series		
210	Remote plotter controller	Connects Teletypewriter and 500 Series plotter to Data-Phone*
211	Remote plotter controller	Connects IBM 1050 or 2741 terminal and 500 Series plotter to Data-Phone
600 Series		
611	Data-Phone transmitter module	Connects CalComp magnetic-tape unit to Data-Phone or coaxial cable
612	Data-Phone transmitter module	Connects CalComp plotter controller to Data-Phone or coaxial cable
621	Remote Data-Phone receiver/plotter controller	Connects any CalComp plotter to Data-Phone or coaxial cable

*The name Data-Phone is a registered trademark of the Bell System.

The product line of CalComp is completed by extensive digital plotter software—both basic software and applications packages—and options and accessories. All the plotters offer plotting on paper, using ball-point or liquid-ink pens; optional accessories for the flatbed plotters include scribing tools, strippable film cutters, and photographic plotting heads to prepare masters for electronics artwork. For the interconnection of different plotting system components, CalComp provides a number of other system components, e.g., the plotter switching adapters for switchable connection of two different plotters to the same computer channel, and core buffers for interface to certain military computers.

APPLICATIONS

CalComp plotters have been used extensively to present the results of scientific experiments in graphical form, to present stock market and business trends, and to prepare graphical management presentations. Other applications include the generation of PERT charts, computer program flow

Table 3-4. Magnetic-Tape Units Available for CalComp Digital Plotting Systems

MODEL NO.	TAPE FORMAT	TAPE ROWS 1 COMMAND	AVAILABLE PLOTTERS	CONNECTION TO PLOTTER	COMMENTS
670	7- or 9-track NRZI	6	500 Series	Direct	Desk-mounted
760	7- or 9-track NRZI	2	500 or 600 Series	Direct	Can be upgraded to 770 or 780†
770	7- or 9-track NRZI	2	Any*	Direct	Can be upgraded to 780†
780	7- or 9-track NRZI	1	Any*	Direct	(Models 760, 770, 780)†
937-7NR	7-track NRZI	1	Any	Via 900 controller	
937-9NR	9-track NRZI	1	Any	Via 900 controller	
937-9PE	9-track, phase-encoded, 1600 bits/inch	1	Any	Via 900 controller	

*Models 770 and 780 magnetic-tape units are also used with the CalComp Model 835 microfilm printer/plotter.

†Models 760, 770, and 780 magnetic-tape units include automatic tape-searching capabilities.

charts, and computer-generated films. In general, drum plotters are used when fairly rapid computer output is needed but accuracy is not paramount; flatbed plotters are more accurate, but also more expensive, than drum plotters of comparable speed. The 700 Series flatbed plotters with photographic or scribing heads have been used to prepare master negatives for electronics artwork; the fast 1136 drum plotter provides quick output of electronics artwork data so that it can be verified prior to photographic plotting.

Besides electronics artwork production a number of other applications are supported by special CalComp software, e.g., subdivision mapping, contouring, schematic drafting, and preparation of plots of three-dimensional surfaces. A recent addition is a garment pattern preparation program in which data for a pattern for one size is processed and produces a succession of different patterns for the different garment sizes.

INPUT REQUIREMENTS

Input requirements for a CalComp digital plotting system depend on the plotter intended. For on-line or remote computer operation, the controlling computer must furnish all commands that operate the plotter; for off-line operation, the input for the plotting operation is taken from data on magnetic tape, paper tape, or cards whose format depends on the particular off-line control and plotter series being used. In the case of off-line plotting systems using the Model 900 controller, the input format also depends on the controller software in use when the plot is generated.

200 Series Remote Plotter Controllers

CalComp offers two controllers for remote on-line plotting applications with 500 Series digital plotters: Model 210 and Model 211. Each of these plotters is connected between the user's terminal, the plotter and the DATA-PHONE®,* or modem, so that the controller directs the passing of data to the user's terminal or to the plotter, as appropriate. The two controllers are the same, but connect to different user terminals: The Model 210 connects to a Teletypewriter, while the Model 211 connects to an IBM 1050 or 2741 terminal. (The IBM 1050 is a time-sharing terminal offering a variety of peripheral devices as options; the 2741 is an IBM Selectric typewriter modified for use by a remote IBM System/360 computer.)

Both the 210 and 211 controllers accept plotting data in an eight-bit character code that is decoded by the controller to form plotter commands; the code specifies plotter, pen, or terminal selection, plotting direction selection and specification of up to 28 plotting steps per character. The 10- or 15-cps transmission lines for which the controllers are designed limits the resulting plotting speed to a maximum of 280 steps per second, compared with the full-rated speed of 300 characters per second for the 500 Series plotters. An optional adapter available for the Model 210 permits 15- or 30-cps input. Housing for the 210 and 211 controllers is provided inside a stand for the plotter to which the controller is connected.

600 Series DATA-PHONE® Adapters

Details of these adapters are given in Table 3-3. With the 600 Series adapters, remote plotting can be performed on-line or off-line, using any permissible combination of CalComp plotting equipment connected either via DATA-PHONES® and a telephone line or (for distances under 5000 feet) by coaxial cable. Unlike the 200 Series of remote plotter controllers, the 600 Series of adapters does not provide for the use of a time-sharing terminal with the remote plotter. Except for the 621 adapter for drum plotters, which is housed in a table-type drum plotter stand, all equipment is housed within the plotter or controller unit to which it is attached.

Model 900 Plotter Controller

The Model 900 plotter controller is a programmed controller for on-line or off-line plotting. It incorporates a special computer designed and built

Table 3-5. Model 900 Controller Features and Options

FEATURE OPTION	DESCRIPTION
Central processor	Over 100 instructions, paged addressing 9-bit bytes, direct memory access channel
Main memory	4,096, 8,192, 16, 384, or 32, 768 bytes, cycle time of 2 microseconds
Plotter interfaces	Compatible with all CalComp digital plotters
Magnetic-tape cartridge	Integrated for program loading and data storage
Teletyprinter	Olivetti keyboard pointer, 19 char./sec
Paper tape reader	300 char./sec
Paper tape punch	120 char./sec (paper); 60 char./sec (mylar)
Card reader	300 cards/min
Seven-channel magnetic tape	Read only, 200/556/800 bits/inch; see Table 3-4
Nine-channel magnetic tape	Read only, 800/1600 bits/inch; see Table 3-4
Disk	CalComp CDI IBM 2311 compatible replaceable disk unit

by CalComp. Characteristics of the Model 900 controller and its optional equipment are summarized in Table 3-5.

The 900 controller is generally used for applications that require sophisticated plotter control. For use of the 900 controller, CalComp provides graphics control software. The standard software operates in the minimum 4096-byte memory and in two modes: line mode, in which line segments can be specified as directives to plot a line from the current pen position to a given position (i.e., linear interpolation); and character mode, in which characters specified by the input data are generated by the software for plotting. Use of this software provides a much more economical tape format as well as an increase in plotting speed, compared with direct off-line plotting without the 900 controller. Off-line plotting with the Model 900 requires the use of the Model 937 magnetic-tape unit; interfaces for on-line use of the Model 900 are available for a number of large computers. Nonstandard software (e.g., interpolation and velocity optimization along curves) has been developed by CalComp for particular customer applications.

MODES OF OPERATION

All CalComp digital plotters operate in an incremental mode. The 700 Series plotters have another mode of operation, which CalComp calls ZIP mode; in this mode, each command causes a velocity increment of the plotting mechanisms. This means that the plotting mechanism need not come to rest after each plotting step, giving faster operation, but controlling software must be used during plotter operation. CalComp provides the Model 900 controller and Models 770 and 780 magnetic-tape units for operation of 700 Series plotters in ZIP mode.

PLOTTING PROCESS

In incremental operation, each plotting command generates signals to the stepping motors to advance the plot one step, and the plotting mechanism comes to rest after each step. The 500 Series plotters have an eight-vector command format in which each step is in one of eight different directions; the other plotters have a 24-vector format, but the 600 Series plotters can also operate in an eight-vector mode for compatibility with the 500 Series command formats. Except for the 500 Series, each plotter

*The name DATA-PHONE® is a registered trademark of the Bell System.

has two different step sizes, which can be changed by a command to the plotter, allowing mixing of step sizes within a single plot.

The 700 Series plotters have a 24-vector format and operate either incrementally or in the ZIP mode described in the preceding paragraph. The operation of plotters in ZIP mode depends either on the software used in the Model 900 controller, discussed next, or on the software used in the computer that generated the magnetic tape for plotting.

SOFTWARE

CalComp provides two kinds of software support for its digital plotting systems: graphic controlling software and host computer software. Graphic controlling software controls the plotting process when it actually takes place, while host computer software prepares data for the plot, whether on line or off line.

The CalComp graphic controlling software consists of complete programs written for the Model 900 controller. This software is stored on cartridge magnetic tape to facilitate loading the controller. Since the Model 900 is the only programmable plotter controller provided by CalComp, no other graphic controlling software is needed; other CalComp plotting systems have hardwired controls.

The host computer basic software is installed in the computer that supplies the plotting data, whether the plotter operates on line or off line. These programs are mainly written in assembly language and FORTRAN, for compatibility with as many computers as possible. The plotting subroutines can also be called from programs written in ALGOL and COBOL. There are three levels of host computer software: (1) basic software, which provides a set of routines for programming basic plotting functions; (2) functional software, which consists of several sets of more elaborate plotting routines that use the basic software and are tailored to particular applications; and (3) applications software, which consists of a series of complete programs for certain plotter applications. The basic software is supplied free of charge to all CalComp plotter customers; the functional and applications software packages are leased separately to users of CalComp digital plotters.

Basic Plotting Software

Basic software consists of an interrelated set of plotting subroutines that prescribe basic plotting operations. These subroutines, which can be readily incorporated into a user's FORTRAN program, initiate and terminate a plot and draw lines, strings of alphanumeric characters, and axes. Moreover, there are capabilities for locating the pen on the plot and for moving it to any specified position. Special characters such as crosses, triangles, and squares can be used for marking the points of a plot. The system maintains an internal cartesian coordinate system so that, after axes have been drawn, further output is specified in terms of the coordinates established. When scaling factors are included in the program, they are automatically introduced by the plotting software.

Functional Software

The functional software is directed more at particular applications than the basic software, but it retains generality. Besides the four separate packages of plotting routines listed in Table 3-6, there are three complete FORTRAN programs: FORGN, for form generation, FLOWCT, for drawing computer program flow charts, and a polynomial curve-fitting program called CRVPT. These three programs each accept parameter cards to define the particular run. Functional software is also available for the output of draft-quality lettering, featuring variable aspect ratio (ratio of character width to height), variable character spacing, and optional left-hand or right-hand italic slanting.

Applications Software

CalComp applications software is a collection of complete programs for particular plotting applications. These programs, written in FORTRAN for compatibility with a large number of different computers, are leased separately to users of CalComp systems. (They can also be used to prepare data for plotting on the CalComp microfilm printer/plotters.)

1. GPCP (General-Purpose Contouring Program): generates a contour map from a data table developed by the user in the computer store. Among the program's applications have been seismic, demographic, geological, and thermal-plots. Special features of the program include the generation of stereoscopic views and the automatic division of large plots into a number of pages of a size specified by the user.

2. THREE-D: automatically generates three-dimensional perspective views from user-generated data in the computer store; it is often used in conjunction with GPCP. With the program, irregularly spaced datum points can be accepted. Other features include user selection of the viewing angle and distance from which a surface is to be drawn, and the inclusion or omission of hidden lines.

3. SYMTRAN: a graphics programming language that makes it easy for

draftsmen and other nonprogrammers to communicate with an automated drawing system. Coding of SYMTRAN follows the draftsman's normal train of thought in planning a drawing. A SYMTRAN user can call on a library of standard symbols or describe new symbols (macros) and recall them as accessions. The SYMTRAN compiler processes all input and produces the plotted graphics, error diagnostics, and program listings.

4. AUTONET (Automatic Network Display): provides the automatic production of PERT and CPM charts from the user's network data. Features of the program include automatic calculation and flagging of the critical

Table 3-6. CalComp Functional Software Packages

PACKAGE	SUBROUTINE	FUNCTION
General	CIRCL	Draws a circle, arc, or spiral
	DASHL	Draws dashed lines between datum points
	DASHP	Draws a dashed line to a specified point
	ELIPS	Draws an ellipse or an elliptical arc
	FIT	Draws a curve through three points
	GRID	Plots a linear grid
	POLY	Draws an equilateral polygon
	RECT	Draws a rectangle of any size
Functional Scientific	CURVX	Plots a function of X over a given range
	CURVY	Plots a function of Y over a given range
	FLINE	Draws a smooth curve through a set of datum points
	LGAXS	Plots an annotated logarithmic axis
	LGLIN	Plots log-log or semilog data
	POLAR	Plots datum points, using polar coordinates
	SCALG	Generates scaling for logarithmic plotting
	SMOOT	Draws a smooth curve through specified datum points
Functional Business	AXISB	Draws an axis with business annotation
	AXISC	Draws an axis with calendar-month annotation
	BAR	Draws bar graphs
	LBAXS	Draws a logarithmic axis with business-oriented annotation
	LGLIN	Plots log-log or semilog data
	SHADE	Draws shading between lines
	SCALG	Generates scaling for logarithmic plotting
Functional Drafting	AROHD	Draws an arrowhead
	ARROW	Draws a line that ends in an arrow
	CNTRL	Draws a centerline
	DIMEN	Draws an annotated dimension line
	LABEL	Draws annotation between specified points

path and of milestone and interface events. All numerical data associated with the timing of each activity is part of the finished plot.

5. SAMPS (Subdivision and Map Plotting System): automates most of the drafting involved in subdivision mapping and planning. Datum points are specified by north and east coordinates; functions of the SAMPS program range from check plotting to production of final maps, e.g., production of working plots for field use, as well as development of road-plan views, accurate overlays for existing maps, and final maps. Diagrams produced with SAMPS have also been used in earthwork calculations.

6. MASKGEN (Integrated Circuit Mask Generator): used for the design and production of integrated circuit masks. Masks are produced using a CalComp flatbed plotter with a strippable film cutter or a photographic plotting head. Design verification plots may be made on a CalComp high-speed drum plotter. Design automation features of the program include generation and use of a library of computer data for frequently used integrated-circuit cells, and automatic chip layout and verification capabilities.

7. FLOWGEN/F (Flowchart Generator/FORTRAN): reads FORTRAN source cards and automatically produces a complete flow chart, drawn and annotated. The package simplifies and standardizes program documentation. Flow charts are precise and uniform; they fit standard 8½x11-inch pages so that they can be stored in a three-ring binder for permanent reference or can be reproduced and distributed for formal program documentation.

8. FINTREN (Financial Trends Chart Generator): produces line or bar charts of ratios important to analysis and decision making in business. Typical charts show such things as net income versus net sales, inventory versus working capital, or fixed assets versus net worth. Data for producing the charts can be taken directly from standard business reports and financial statements. The program charts activities over any period up to 36 months. Automatic scaling capabilities are included.

9. SCOPLT (Scope Plot): used to produce hard copies of any image presented on an IBM 2250 display unit. It satisfies the need for documentation with clean, accurate, and reproducible copies. In addition, the program includes automatic diagnostic checks and corresponding error codes.

OPTIONS

Various optional marking kits for the CalComp digital plotters provide liquid-ink and ball-point pen marking for all the plotters (see Table 3-7). Other options include strippable-film cutting tools and photographic plotting equipment as described next.

There are two strippable film cutters: a four-tool cutter for use on the

Table 3-7. CalComp Marking Kits

			APPLICABLE PLOTTERS*	
KIT MODEL NO.	PEN TYPE	PLOTTING TYPE	PLOTTERS (KIT STANDARD)	PLOTTERS (KIT OPTIONAL)
20-300	Liquid ink	General-Purpose	None	500 Series, 600 Series
10065-101	Liquid ink	High-speed	None	700 Series
10070-101	Combination liquid-ink/ ball-point	High-speed	700 Series	700 Series
10073-101	Combination liquid-ink/ ball-point	General-purpose	502, 600 Series	500 Series, 600 Series
10082-101	Ball-point	General-purpose and high-speed	563, 565, 575	Any

*The 1136 drum plotter is not included.

large plotting tables, and a single-tool cutter used on the small flatbed or drum plotters. The strippable film cutters use tungsten carbide blades to cut in any of eight different directions; an omnidirectional cutting tool is provided for arcs and nonstandard angles. The depth of cutting is finely adjustable so that the film base is undamaged.

The Model 7180 optical writing system provides photographic plotting capabilities for the precision flatbed plotting tables. Light generated by a solid-state luminescent panel passes through an aperture (which is an etched metal disk) into a fiber optics bundle whose end rests lightly on the plotting surface, eliminating any need for focusing. The optics system permits the cross section of the light beam to be demagnified 1, 2, 5, 10, or 20 times as it passes through the fiber optics bundle; there are eight program-selectable bundles with interchangeable apertures.

The optical writing system consists of a plotting head and a separate control electronics unit. The plotting head for the optical writing system contains the eight fiber optics bundles. Aperture sizes (before demagnification) vary from 0.005 to 0.374 inch in diameter for circles and up to 0.260 inch on a side for rectangles and squares. With this system there are 85 standard apertures; the customer may specify a nonstandard aperture, provided it fits within a circle of 0.374-inch diameter. Apertures in the plotting head can be easily changed by the operator. Operation is in a flashing mode, the electroluminescent panel being pulsed once for each step of 0.01 inch; the first and last exposures of a line are intensified to avoid underexposure. Characteristics of the optical writing system are summarized in Table 3-8.

Table 3-8. Characteristics of the CalComp Optical Writing System

CHARACTERISTIC	SPECIFICATION
Operating speeds	
With Model 738	286 inches/min
With Model 638	76.5 inches/min
With Model 745	255 inches/min
Apertures	
Round aperture line width	0.005–0.374-inch diameter
Square aperture line width	0.005–0.260-inch per side
Line width tolerance	
Round and square apertures	Up to 1% of line width, or 0.0005 inch
Fiber optics bundle	
Dimensions	2 inches long; 0.4-inch diameter (entrance) Exit diameters: 0.4 inch at 1X minification 0.2 inch at 2X minification 0.08 inch at 5X minification 0.04 inch at 10X minification 0.02 inch at 20X minification
System dimensions	
Light-pen assembly	8¾ inches wide by 4¾ inches deep by 7 inches high
Electronics control	28 inches wide by 19 inches deep by 9⅝ inches high
Weight	
Light-pen assembly	4 lb
Electronics control	35 lb

4. DRUM-TYPE PLOTTERS

INTRODUCTION

An important section of the total digital plotter market is represented by drum-type plotters in which the plot is produced by the combined movements of a pen carriage across the plotting surface and a backward and forward motion of the plotting medium itself. Drum-type plotters are notable for their low cost and high speed in comparison with flatbed plotters; disadvantages are somewhat lower accuracy and reduced scope for the use of special plotting tools and media.

In general, drum-type plotters operate incrementally (the Gerber drum plotter, mentioned later, is an exception). Incremental operation means that relatively unsophisticated control of the plotting process is required so that a drum plotter can connect in a fairly simple manner to a computer (local or remote) without the need for an expensive interface. Refer to Chapter 2 for a general discussion of plotting techniques. There are two principal types of drum plotters currently available: small, low-cost units intended primarily for use as computer output devices in business or scientific applications, and the large, fast drum plotters whose principal application is for electronics artwork verification.

CalComp pioneered the low-cost drum plotter and is the leader in that area, offering the product line discussed in Chapter 3. Other important suppliers of drum plotting systems are Houston Instrument, with its COMPLOT® line, University Computing (UCC), and Auto-trol.

In terms of the number of devices sold, drum-type plotters are by far the most important sector of the digital plotter market, since they provide a low-cost, general-purpose graphics output capability for the general-purpose computer installation. Diversified applications have developed, ranging from the straightforward graphical presentation of computer output in business or scientific applications to such specialized areas as the production of weather maps, masters for business forms, artwork, or architectural and engineering drawings.

A newer and more limited market segment is represented by larger, faster devices that generate plots on paper at high speed (up to 1600 inches per minute), with accuracies comparable to those of many flatbed plotters. These models have been developed largely to produce verification plots of data prepared for the photographic plotting of electronics artwork masters on flatbed plotters. They also suit any application that requires production of large quantities of graphical output on paper; the fact that the paper is in a long roll means that operation can continue for long periods unattended, making the systems ideal for plotting service bureaus.

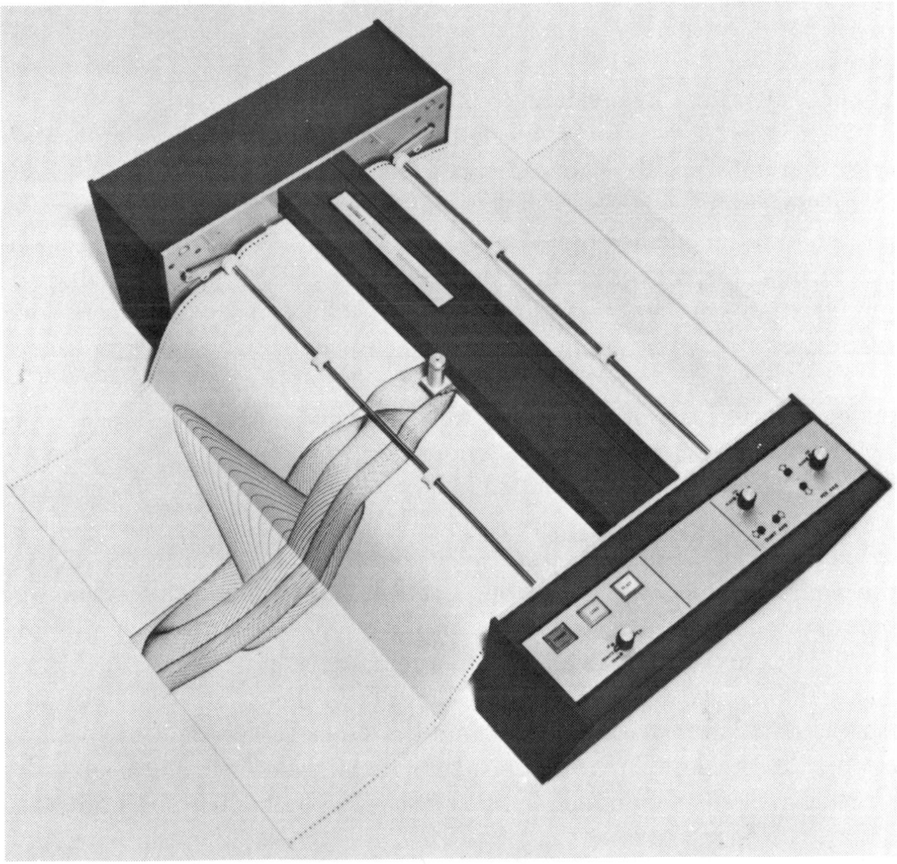

Fig. 4-1. Houston Instrument DP-3 digital plotter.

Three of these plotters currently available are the CalComp 1136, described in the preceding chapter, the UCC Series 2000, and the Gerber Scientific Model 62. The last is the fastest to date and uses a nonincremental plotting technique, which makes it compatible with the complete range of Gerber automatic drafting systems discussed in the next chapter.

Three companies and their products are discussed in this chapter: the Houston Instrument COMPLOT® digital plotting system,* the UCC incremental plotters, and the Auto-trol Model 6035 digital plotter, which offers both drum and flatbed plotting capabilities and paves the way to the discussion of flatbed digital plotting systems covered in Chapter 5.

HOUSTON INSTRUMENT COMPLOT® DIGITAL PLOTTING SYSTEMS

General Description

The Houston Instrument COMPLOT® plotters, Models DP-1, DP-3 (Fig. 4-1), DP-5, and DP-12, are all drum-type plotters in which sprocket-fed paper passes beneath a beam that supports a moving pen assembly. Stepwise movements of both the pen and paper enable a plot to be generated by successive steps in any of eight different directions.

Each step (or pen up/down movement) is specified by a single character of input data, the pen and paper coming to rest after the step. Fanfold paper, which these plotters normally use, is fed from a pile behind the plotter, and the finished plot emerges at the front. A ball-point or felt-tip pen is used to plot on fanfold paper; higher-quality plots, suitable for reproduction, can be produced on mylar or vellum, using an optional pen that draws a very fine line with India ink. Since mylar and vellum cannot be fanfolded, these media require optional roll-feed attachments. The main characteristics of the four plotters are listed in Table 4-1.

Except for the DP-12 plotter, which can connect directly to a data set for remote (time sharing) operation, the COMPLOT® plotters are designed for on-line computer use, and are connected to a computer input/output channel via interface electronics provided either by Houston Instrument or by the computer manufacturer. Four controls are available for off-line or remote digital plotting. The PTC-4 and BTC-7/200 controls offer plotting capabilities for a time-sharing link to a remote computer, while the MTR-2 and MTR-9 controls provide off-line digital plotting from magnetic tape. Characteristics of the controls are summarized in Table 4-2.

Besides the digital plotters and controls, Houston Instrument provides an extensive range of digital plotter software, including both basic plotting

*The name COMPLOT® is the registered trademark of Houston Instrument.

subroutines and complete packages for particular plotting applications. These are sold to users of other digital plotting systems as well as to those who have COMPLOT® series units.

Applications

The Houston Instrument COMPLOT® plotters are suitable for innumerable plotting applications that are compatible with the inherent accuracy of drum plotters and are essentially limited only by the plotter width of the particular COMPLOT® model in use and the restriction of the series to the plotting mediums of fanfold paper, mylar, and vellum. The ability to produce plots as long as a single package of fanfold paper (144 feet) is an advantage in many applications.

Houston Instrument software includes packages for general plotting, drawing graphs, generation of overall views and perspective drawings of three-dimensional surfaces, drawing of contour maps, output of computer program flow charts and PERT diagrams, generation of business-form layouts, piping diagrams, architectural drawings, and weather maps.

Table 4-1. Characteristics of COMPLOT® DIGITAL PLOTTERS

PLOTTER	WIDTH OF PLOT, INCHES	STEPS PER SECOND	FULL MODEL NUMBER	STEP SIZE	COMMENTS
DP-1	11	300	DP-1-1	0.010 inch	Plotter step size is
			DP-1-5	0.005 inch	changed at the
			DP-1-M1	0.10 mm	factory for fee of
			DP-1-M2	0.25 mm	$150.
DP-3	22	300 or	DP-3-1	0.010 inch	Step size can be changed
		400*	DP-3-5	0.005 inch	between 0.010/0.005
			DP-3-M1	0.10 mm	inch or between 0.25/
			DP-3-M2	0.25 mm	0.10 mm by the operator.
DP-5	11	1200	DP-5-5	0.005 inch	Once chosen, the step size
			DP-5-2	0.0025 inch	is fixed for a particular plotter.
DP-12	11	300	DP-12-1	0.010 inch	Once chosen, the step size
			DP-12-5	0.005 inch	is fixed for a particular
			DP-12-M1	0.10 mm	plotter; unit is operable
			DP-12-M2	0.25 mm	with 2000-baud or 2400-baud data set.

*The DP-3 plotter offers two different models, each with two switch-selectable step sizes. For either model, the stepping rate is 300 steps per second for the larger step size and 400 steps per second for the smaller step size.

Input Requirements

Plotter input consists of a series of pulses to control not only the motions of the paper-and-pen assembly but also the raising and lowering of the pen. If the plotter is operated on line to a computer, the input is taken directly from the computer output channel via interface electronics.

For remote (time sharing) use, the plotter is connected to a PTC-4 or BTC-7/200 control. Note that the DP-12 plotter can be connected to a data set. For off-line plotting, the MTR-2 and MTR-9 controls are available. See Table 4-2.

The PTC-4 and MTR-9 controllers both offer two features that add significantly to the speed and efficiency of their operation. They include a buffer memory, which means that input data can be received asynchronously with plotting and leads to more efficient utilization of the communications line (PTC-4) or magnetic-tape unit (MTR-9), and also can accept data for the end points of a straight line, internally generating the steps needed for this. The last feature leads to significant savings both in data transmission time (PTC-4) and in the compactness of plotting data on magnetic tape (MTR-9). Houston Instrument distinguishes the feature by the trade name END-STEP®.

1. *The* PTC-4 *plotter/typewriter controller.* This device is a desk-mounted unit that provides control for a Teletypewriter and a COMPLOT digital plotter attached to a time-sharing link. Normally, the DP-1 and DP-3 plotters, which have a rated speed of 300 steps per second, are used with the PTC-4; but the PTC-4 can optionally be modified to accommodate a DP-5 plotter, which has a rated speed of 1200 increments per second. The PTC-4 incorporates a buffer memory and linear interpolation, both of which

Table 4-2. COMPLOT® Digital Plotting System Controls

CONTROL	FUNCTION	APPLICABLE PLOTTERS	COMMENTS
PTC-4	Time-sharing plotting	DP-1	Buffered operation and END-STEP® mode (see text)*
BTC-7/200	Adds graphic output to CDC 200 user terminal	DP-1; DP-3	
MTR-2	Off-line plotting from magnetic tape	DP-1; DP-3; DP-5	
MTR-9	Off-line plotting from magnetic tape	DP-1; DP-3; DP-5	Buffered operation and END-STEP mode (see text)

*Mode END STEP is a registered trademark of Houston Instrument.

significantly increase the efficiency of remote plotting compared to direct connection of the plotter to a communications line, as discussed earlier.

2. *The* BTC-7/200 *plotting system.* The BTC-7/200 adds a plotting capability to the CDC 200 user terminal, which is a programmed data communications terminal, by providing an interface between the line printer channel of the CDC 200 and a DP-1 or DP-3 plotter. The Houston Instrument plotting software can be used with the CDC computer to which the CDC 200 is remotely attached. The BTC-7/200 can be easily added to a CDC 200 in the field.

3. *The* MTR-2 *off-line digital plotting system.* The MTR-2 provides an incremental magnetic-tape reader and an interface for a DP-1, DP-3, or DP-5 plotter. Characteristics of the magnetic-tape unit used are given in Table 4-3.

4. *The* MTR-9 *off-line digital plotting system.* The MTR-9 provides a Mohawk magnetic-tape deck and interface for a DP-1, DP-3, or DP-5 plotter. The buffering and END-STEP® features discussed earlier are included in this unit. Characteristics of the tape unit used are given in Table 4-3. The COMPLOT® digital plotters operate only in an incremental mode, in which the pen and paper stop moving after each command.

Plotting Process

Each plotter command either raises and lowers the pen or moves the pen carriage and paper so as to generate a line one step long in one of eight

Table 4-3. Magnetic-Tape Unit Characteristics for MTR-2 and MTR-9 Controllers

CHARACTERISTICS	MTR-2	MTR-9
IBM-compatible tape	Yes	Yes
Recording densities, bits/inch*	200; 556; 800	800
7-track tape	200; 556; 800	800
9-track tape	800	800
Reel diameter, inches	10.5	10.5
Tape speeds, inches/sec		
Reading	1.5	Reads blocks of characters
Seaching, block advance	8.0	10
Rewinding	100	50
Automatic tape search	No	Yes
END-STEP	No	Yes
Buffered reading	No	Yes

*One tape width and density must be specified at the time of ordering.

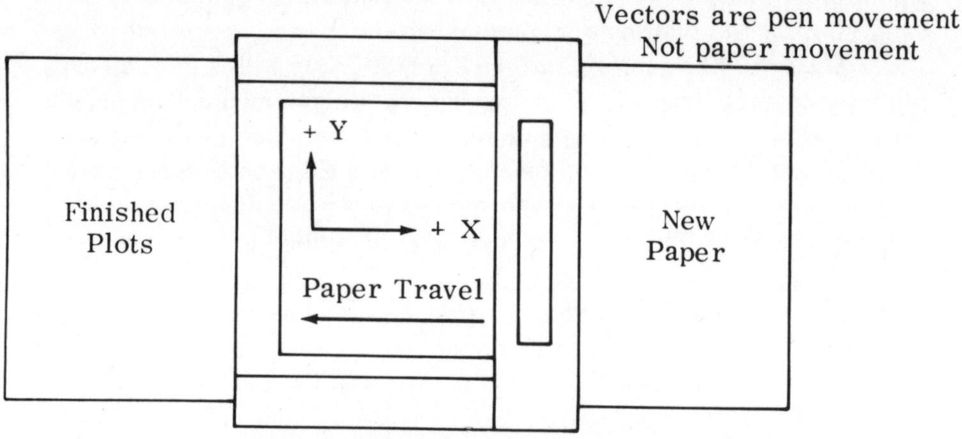

Fig. 4-2. Motions of pen and paper during operation of COMPLOT® digital plotters.

directions. Figure 4-2 shows the ways in which the pen and paper move during operation. For a general discussion of plotting, see Chapter 2.

Software

Houston Instrument software is installed in the computer that supplies the plotting data, whether the plotter operates on line or off line. Written largely in FORTRAN II and FORTRAN IV, these programs are compatible with a large number of computers.

The software repertoire falls into two classes: (1) basic software, which provides a set of routines for the programming of basic plotting functions, and (2) the more sophisticated and specialized plotting routines and programs designed for particular applications. A nominal fee of $50 is charged for the basic software to defray the cost of the cards or tape. The plotting packages are sold separately to users of other digital plotters as well as to users of COMPLOT® plotters.

Basic Plotting Software

Basic software consists of an interrelated set of plotting subroutines that prescribe basic plotting operations. These subroutines can be readily incorporated into a user's FORTRAN program. Subroutines are included for initiating and terminating a plot and for drawing lines, alphanumeric characters, and axes. There are capabilities for locating the pen on the plot and for moving it to any specified position. Special characters such as crosses, triangles, and squares can be used for marking the points of a plot. The system maintains an internal cartesian coordinate system so that, after the drawing of axes, further output is specified in terms of the coordinates established. When scaling factors are included in the program, they are automatically introduced by the plotting system.

Plotting Systems

HI-FLOW SYSTEM. The Houston Instrument Hi-Flow system is a software package for the generation of flow charts and is intended mainly for the COMPLOT plotters. The program accepts as input a standard FORTRAN card deck, preceded by a control card, and generates a flow chart of the program as output. The program can also generate a reformatted version of the input card deck, eliminating spurious blanks and reorganizing statement numbering, which enhances the readability of the FORTRAN source coding.

CPM-PLOT SYSTEM. The CPM-Plot system is a software package for the generation of PERT time networks via digital plotter and is designed primarily for use with the COMPLOT® series. It is available in two versions: (1) activity-oriented, in which work descriptions are placed along the activity lines, and (2) event-oriented, in which the work descriptions are placed within the event boxes.

Input for CPM-plot is taken from a user's PERT/TIME activity report file in a standard format on magnetic tape. A variety of activity and event symbols are used to signify the current status of the activities shown. Houston Instrument states that the use of the package provides significant time and cost advantages over the drawing of PERT networks by hand.

TRIDEM® SYSTEM.* The TRIDEM package is an extensive collection of routines for the plotting of three-dimensional surface data on a digital plotter and is mainly intended for use with the COMPLOT plotters. It is a complete program that accepts data either in the form of a table of the values of a function of two variables or as a set of coordinates of points on a three-dimensional surface, each specified by three-dimensional cartesian coordinates. Output may be a three-dimensional, stereo, or perspective plot of the data.

Options include the exclusion of "hidden" lines in three-dimensional plots, the construction of three-dimensional and perspective plots of the surface as seen from any angle, and the production of stereoscopic plots for viewing with two-colored glasses or an optical stereoscope. If required, annotations added to the graph can be included in the three-dimensional plot with the appropriate perspective and angle of view, to enhance the

*The name TRIDEM® is a registered trademark of Houston Instrument.

three-dimensional effect of the presentation. The TRIDEM system includes a feature for the automatic smoothing of lines in drawings that would otherwise be ragged because of the lack of data; the amount of interpolation performed by the program is selectable by the user.

CONTOUR-PLOT® SYSTEM.* This system is a software package that enables digital plotter preparation of contour maps of three-dimensional surfaces, and is mainly intended for use with the COMPLOT plotters. Besides providing annotation, interpolation, and contouring capabilities, the system allows the user of the package to insert his own coding for manipulation of the input data. A number of options are available for the basic package, which provides additional data manipulation functions; these are described in Table 4-4.

Subroutines

UTILITY DRAFTING PACKAGE. The utility drafting package is a collection of subroutines generally applicable to drafting. It provides for the drawing of dimension lines on diagrams and insertion of arrowheads and annotation. Dashed-line features are also included.

GENERAL GRAPHICS PACKAGE. This package contains a number of additional subroutines of general graphical application, including routines for

Table 4-4. Optional Features of the Contour-Plot Software System

FEATURE	CAPABILITIES
Multiple surface operations	Plotting of sum, product, difference, quotient, union, or intersection of two or more surfaces.
Area and volume computation	Computation of areas and volumes specified by contours or by user-specified polygonal curves.
Single profile plotting	Plotting of a specified cross section of a surface.
Multiple profile plotting	Plotting of multiple profiles with perspective effects optionally included.
Interpolation	Plotting of discontinuous data; for example, data produced by a fault. Interpolation over gradient discontinuities can also be specified.
Data refinement	Changes grid spacing, effects data smoothing (filtering).
Trend analysis	Computation of trend surfaces.
Printer contouring	Contour output on a line printer.
Isometric diagrams	Provides a feature for the construction of isometric diagrams.

*The name CONTOUR-PLOT® is a registered trademark of Houston Instrument.

the generation of circular and elliptical arcs, the construction and (optional) shading of rectangles and regular polygons, and curve fitting.

Options

For high-quality plotting suitable for reproduction, the DP-1, DP-3, and DP-12 plotters can use mylar or vellum. Two options are needed: a marking kit, which allows the use of pens for plotting; and a roll-chart adapter, which permits the use of media that cannot be fanfolded (mylar and vellum). These options are unavailable for the fast DP-5 plotter because a pen cannot operate satisfactorily at its higher speed (1200 steps per second); however, a marking kit for the DP-5 is available, which offers a greater choice of ball-point and fiber-tip pens than those provided as standard equipment. The model numbers of the roll-chart adapters and marking kits available for the different plotter models are given in Table 4-5.

Table 4-5. Model Numbers of Options for COMPLOT® Digital Plotters

PLOTTER	ROLL CHART ADAPTER	MARKING KIT
DP-1	RC-1	MK-15
DP-3	RC-3	MK-31
DP-5	Not available	MK-50
DP-12	RC-1	MK-15

Roll-Chart Adapters

The RC-1 and RC-3 adapters provide supply and take-up rollers for the plotting medium and are field installable on existing plotters. There are three operating positions: The rollers may be next to the plotter, removed from the plotter so that 49½ inches of the plotting medium are visible, or folded away from the plotter so that fanfold paper can be used conventionally.

Marking Kits

The MK-15 and MK-31 kits provide plotting in India ink. Four different ink colors and four different pen-tip diameters (from 0.2 to 0.5 mm) are included. The pens are intended for plotting on mylar or vellum; plotting with these pens on fanfold paper is not recommended because priming wires at the tips of the pens catch in the fanfold perforations and cause tearing.

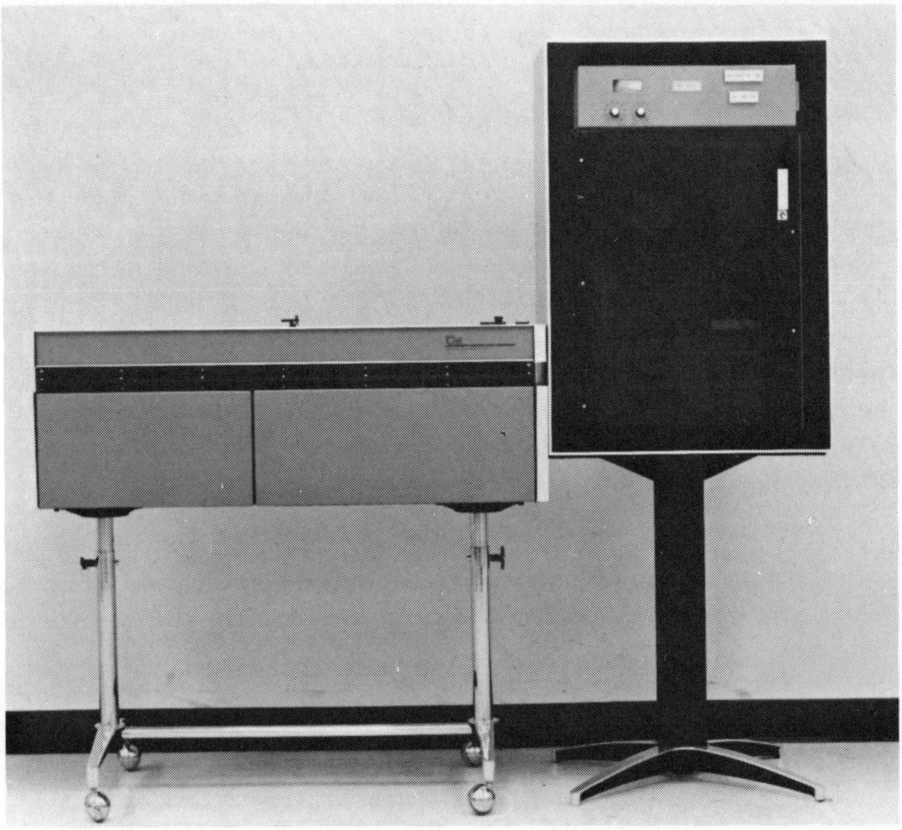

M-2000 magnetic-tape control.

UNIVERSITY COMPUTING INCREMENTAL PLOTTERS

General Description

The UCC incremental drum plotters (Fig. 4-3) comprise the Series 1430, 300, and 2000 plotters for low-speed, medium-speed, and high-speed plotting, respectively (see Table 4-6). These instruments generate the plot as a series of steps, each step being in one of eight different directions. The plotting steps are effected by the combined movements of the drum, which carries the sprocketed paper, and the pen carriage, which moves from side to side across the plot. The plotters are primarily intended for plotting on paper with ball-point, fiber-tip, or liquid-ink pens; nevertheless, capabilities for plotting on mylar are optionally available for the entire series. Other options for the Series 300 and Series 2000 plotters include a choice of paper widths and facilities to display the plot being generated.

Table 4-6. UCC On-Line Incremental Plotters

SERIES	MODEL	STEP LENGTH	STEPS PER SECOND
300	331	0.010 inch	300
	345	0.005 inch	400
1430	1431	0.010 inch	250
	1435	0.005 inch	300
	1431m	0.1 mm	300
	1432m	0.2 mm	300
2000	2000	0.0025 inch*	800/1200/1600/ 2000†

*Quoted step length refers to on-line use; step length in off-line use is program-selectable.
†Stepping rate of a Series 2000 plotter is selectable manually or by program.

The UCC incremental low-speed plotters are primarily intended for on-line computer use via a computer interface. Off-line plotting systems using magnetic-tape, card, or paper-tape input are available for the Series 2000 plotter (see Table 4-7).

Extensive application software furnished by UCC comprises basic and functional plotting subroutines and complete plotting programs for contouring, three-dimensional surfaces, graphs, PERT charts, and computer program flow charts.

Applications

The UCC incremental plotters are suitable for innumerable plotting applications that are compatible with the inherent accuracy of drum plotters; they are limited only by a specific plotter's width and the plotting media of fanfold paper and mylar. The ability to produce plots as long as a single roll of paper (100 feet for Series 300 and Series 2000, 160 feet for

Table 4-7. UCC Off-Line Incremental Plotting Systems

MODEL	INPUT MEDIUM	RATED SPEED
M-2007	Magnetic tape (7-track)	(1)
M-2009	Magnetic tape (9-track)	(1)
C-2000	Punched card	200 cards/min
P-2000	Punched tape	300 char./sec

Note (1): M-2007 offers magnetic-tape recording densities of 556 or 800 bits per inch; M-2009 offers a tape-recording density of 800 bits per inch. Tape speeds in both cases are 2.5 inches per second for reading, 20 inches per second for searching, and 37.5 inches per second for rewinding.

Series 1430) is an advantage in many applications. Particular application areas cited by UCC include—

1. Engineering drawings.
2. Engineering design.
3. Scientific/equation plotting.
4. Business graphs and bar charts.
5. Road mapping.
6. Contouring (geodetic survey).
7. Aerial photogrammetry.
8. Verification of tapes for numerically controlled machine tools.
9. PERT charting.
10. Program documentation (flow charting of FORTRAN programs).
11. Property layouts (including subdivision).
12. Generation of originals for business forms.

Digital plotter applications are discussed in Chapter 2.

Input Requirements

When UCC incremental plotters are used on line, input consists of a series of commands, each of which either causes the pen to be raised/lowered or the plot to be advanced by a single step in one of the eight stepping directions. The Series 2000 plotter also accepts commands to set the stepping rate at 800, 1200, 1600, or 2000 steps per second.

Additional commands are available when plotting is performed off line via the M-2007, M-2009, C-2000, or P-2000 off-line digital plotting systems (see Table 4-7). With these commands, the step length can be set to 0.00025, 0.005, or 0.010 inch, and up to 1023 plotting steps per command can be specified. These capabilities compress data for economical use of the off-line plotting medium and cause a sequence of steps to be generated by the controller. For example, when the step length is specified at 0.005 inch, the off-line controller passes each subsequent plotting step command to the plotter twice, with an advance of 0.0025 inch at each command. Additionally, the drawing of a line up to 1023 steps long can be specified with a single command; this mode of operation, which UCC calls DELTA® mode,* is discussed in the following paragraphs. Since the off-line plotting systems are not buffered, magnetic-tape reading is not overlapped with plotting.

Modes of Operation

The UCC incremental plotters operate only in an incremental mode; that

*The name DELTA® is a registered trademark of University Computing Company.

is, the pen and paper stop moving after each command. The DELTA® mode for the Series 2000 off-line systems is a data-compression device only; during the execution of a DELTA® mode command, the plotter still advances in a series of single steps. This technique may be compared with linear interpolation features of some more elaborate competitive plotters in which line drawing takes place in a single plotting movement.

Plotting Process

Each plotter command either raises and lowers the pen or moves the pen carriage and paper so that a line one step long is generated in one of eight directions.

For a general discussion of plotting, see Chapter 2.

Software

Three levels of software coverage are provided by UCC for the generation of plotting data: (1) standard software, a series of subroutines for basic plotting applications; (2) functional software, a collection of subroutines of a higher and more specialized level than those provided as part of the standard software; (3) applications software, complete computer programs for particular plotting applications. Most of the software is written in FORTRAN for compatibility with many computers. A special version of the standard software for IBM 1130 and 1800 computers provides facilities roughly equivalent to the general package and is also compatible with IBM 1130 and 1800 software. All UCC software is provided free of charge to users of UCC plotters.

STANDARD SOFTWARE. Standard software consists of an interrelated set of plotting subroutines that can be readily incorporated into a FORTRAN program and used to prescribe basic plotting operations. These subroutines can initiate and terminate a plot and draw lines, circular arcs, alphanumeric characters, and axes. There are capabilities for locating the pen on the plot and for moving it to any specified position. Other facilities include data conversion and alteration of the plotter step size and speed (for use with Series 2000 plotters).

The system maintains an internal cartesian coordinate system so that, after axes have been drawn, further output is specified in terms of the coordinates established. When scaling factors are included in the program, they are automatically implemented by the plotting system.

FUNCTIONAL SOFTWARE. The functional software consists of a collection of FORTRAN subroutines that use the standard software and provide more specialized and sophisticated plotting functions. The functional software subroutines are grouped into five applications areas: general, symbolic, scientific, business, and drafting (see Table 4-8).

APPLICATIONS SOFTWARE. Five plotting applications programs are

Table 4-8. UCC Functional Software

APPLICATION AREA	SUBROUTINE	DESCRIPTION
General	BUBLE	Sorts plot data
	DOTLN	Plots dotted straight line
	RECT	Draws any rectangle at any orientation
	REPOL	Draws a regular polygon with specific number of sides, center, radius, and orientation
	SHADE	Shades specified region with straight lines of specified spacing and orientation
	SIMUL	Finds point of intersection of two lines
Symbolic	ELECT	Draws specified electrical symbol
	GEO	Draws specified geological symbol
	GRAF	Plots selected symbol at data point
	GREEK	Draws specified Greek letter
	LILET	Draws specified lower-case letter
	MAP	Draws specified map symbol
	MATH	Draws specified math symbol
	POWER	Draws specified power symbol
	WELD	Draws specified welding symbol
Scientific	ELIPS	Draws ellipse or elliptical arc
	FUNCUV	Curve-fitting subroutine
	POLAR	Plots curve specified in polar coordinates
	EST	General-purpose estimation subroutine; uses Newton-Raphson method
	INTRP	Interpolates, linear or quadratic
	POL	Plots polar coordinate system
	MAXMN	Finds and plots maxima and minima of data arrays
Business	BAR	Plots a bar chart
	CALAN	Plots an axis with months marked
	GRID	Draws a rectilinear grid
	HIST	Plots a histogram
	PIE	Draws a pie chart
Drafting	ARROW	Draws a line with arrowhead at either end, or at both ends
	CENLN	Plots a centerline
	DASH	Draws a dashed line
	DIMS	Draws a dimension line
	DIMLN	Draws and annotates a dimension line

offered by UCC: contouring, three-dimensional plotting, data presentation, and output of PERT charts and computer program flow charts.

The contour program provides the capability to plot a contour map of a surface defined by randomly spaced datum points. A grid network is constructed by the program, and interpolation is used to produce smooth contours.

Three-dimensional projections of single-valued surfaces are generated by an applications program whose capabilities include the preparation of isometric, oblique, perspective, and stereoscopic views of a specified surface. Other uses of the program include drawing and labeling of axes, interpolation, and variable scaling.

A PERT network can be plotted on a UCC plotter from a user's data file, using an applications package whose capabilities include identification of the critical path. Four types of event blocks are included in the standard package: normal, optional, interface, and terminal. Each event can be further identified as expected, scheduled, or actual. Activity descriptions, expected dates, and slack times are also specified.

The package that generates flow charts of FORTRAN programs can also generate a new card deck of the input program in a more readable format so that statements of the original program are renumbered sequentially and a cross-reference list is provided.

Options

Optional plotting kits available for all UCC incremental plotters offer plotting with felt-tip, ball-point, or liquid-ink pens. In addition, kits for plotting on mylar are available for the Series 300 and 2000 plotters.

Standard paper width for the Series 300 and 2000 plotters is 30 inches, with a plotting width of 29 inches; optional adapters for these plotters allow the use of 12-inch paper, which has a plotting width of 10.5 inches. Also available for the Series 300 and 200 plotters, with either paper width, are plot-display attachments, which let the operator view the plot as it is being generated.

Options available for the Series 2000 plotters only are an elapsed time meter, registering the total time for which the plotter has been turned on; a paper cutter; and a switch, for changing the plotter from on-line to off-line operation, or vice versa.

AUTO-TROL MODEL 6035 DIGITAL PLOTTER

General Description

Auto-trol Model 6035 digital plotter (Fig. 4-4) is a high-speed, X-Y coordinate plotter containing both flatbed and drum-style plotting surfaces. Its drum plotting mechanism, essentially a duplication of the Auto-trol 6040 plotter, executes an increment size of 0.0005 inch and operates at a line-drawing speed of 10 inches per second in any direction. Its flatbed plotter is accurate to ∓0.004 inch and is offered with plotting surfaces as large as 60 x 60 inches.

A number of optional features are available, including a 62-character mechanical printer, an eight-pen turret, a directional scriber and cutter, a CRT display, and a camera for photographing the display.

There are two principal plotter component groupings: (1) the control components (control electronics plus register displays, operator controls, and read-in devices), which are combined in a floor-mounted console; and (2) the plotting components (drum, plotting heads, and table).

The carriage of the 6035 plotter series can carry any two functions at the same time, i.e., printer-and-pen turret, two printers, standard tool holder, and printer. There is a 2½-inch offset between the two function positions. Complete program control for swapping between these two function positions is a standard feature.

Applications

Since it offers both drum and flatbed printing surfaces, the Auto-trol Model 6035 is versatile. The drum surface is particularly effective for long strip plots; the flatbed is available for sizes that will fit on the plotting surface and, of course, is required when the plot is made on a material that is not suitable for drum plotting. According to the manufacturer, it is suited for all forms of automated drawing, ranging from missile orbits to printed-circuit artwork.

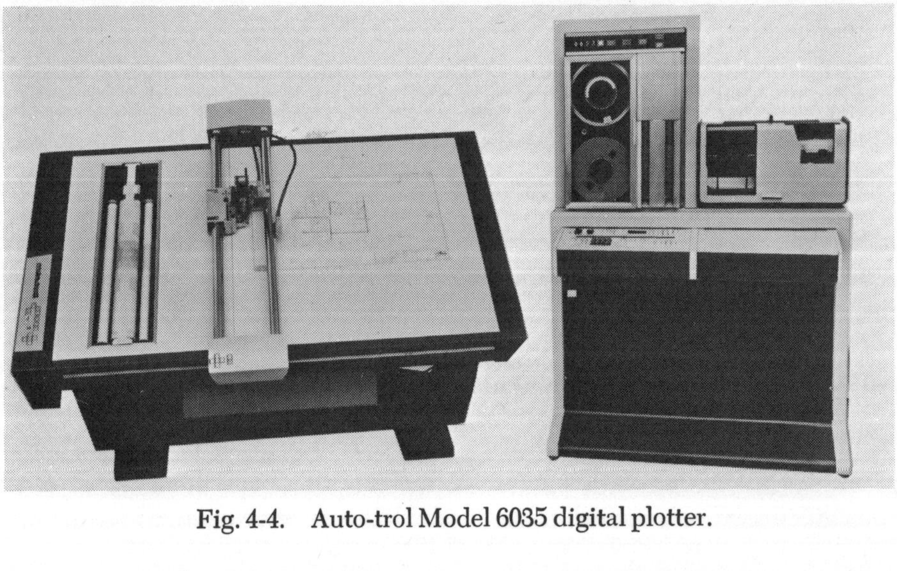

Fig. 4-4. Auto-trol Model 6035 digital plotter.

Table 4-9. Automatic Input Devices

DEVICE	MODEL	INPUT MEDIUM	INPUT CODE	READING SPEED
Paper-tape reader	5200	8-channel punched paper tape	EIA or ASC II	500 char./sec
Card reader	5000	Punched cards	Hollerith	400 cards/min
Magnetic-tape reader	5707	7-track, 0.5-inch mag tape	IBM-compatible	27½ inches/sec
Magnetic-tape reader	5709	9-track, 0.5-inch mag tape	IBM-compatible	27½ inches/sec
Computer interfaces	various*	Direct computer output		

*Available for various computers.

Input Requirements

Four of the automatic input devices listed in Table 4-9 can connect to the console for instant availability upon operator command. In addition, the operator can enter data manually via the console keyboard; and if the optional 6030.03 printer is installed, legends typed at the keyboard will appear on the output drawing. Other entries may also be made at the console, some providing for routine operation and others directly affecting the operating mode. The latter are—

1. READ NEXT *instruction*: permits the operator to read the next instruction into the register for verification before execution.
2. *Pen control*: used to place the pen in up, down, or automatic position.
3. *Velocity control*: permits operator adjustment of plotting velocity from ½ to 10 inches per second.
4. *Mirror image*: permits operator to specify the plotting of a mirror image of the input data.
5. *Axis rotation*: allows the operator to rotate the axes of the plot 90 degrees.
6. *Scale*: lets the operator specify a 1:1, ½:1, or 2:1 scale factor.
7. *Manual position*: provides for manually controlled carriage motion.

Modes of Operation

The Auto-trol Model 6035 digital plotter (Fig. 4-5) can automatically operate in the following modes without installation of any optional equipment:

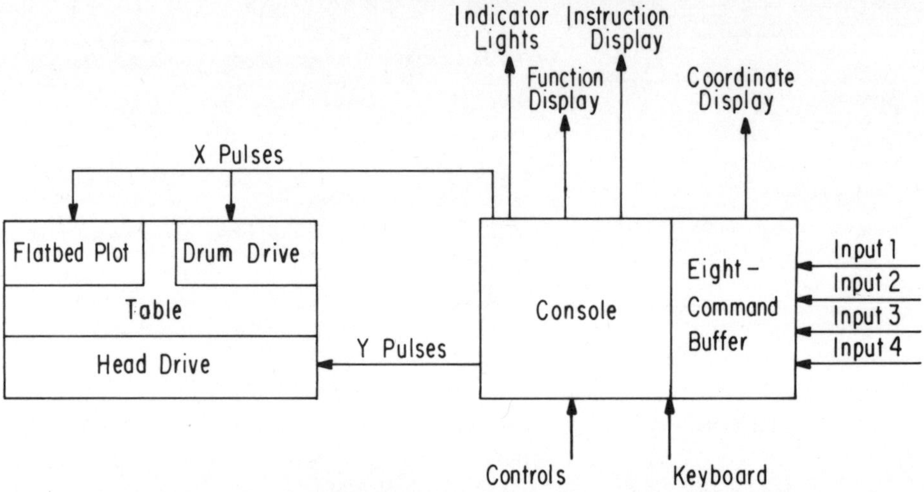

Fig. 4-5. System flow, Auto-trol Model 6035 plotter.

1. Move plotting mechanism to new X- and Y-coordinates with pen up (nonwriting).
2. Move plotting mechanism to new X- and Y-coordinates with pen down (writing in line-drawing mode).
3. Maintain constant plotting speed as long as input data is available. This mode, called SCOOT by the manufacturer, increases throughput by eliminating both the deceleration that normally occurs as a plot point is approached and the acceleration that normally occurs as a plot point is left. This mode, of course, cannot be used when the plotted curve is so sharp that the follower is unable to trace it at a constant speed.
4. Draw a dashed line.
5. Draw a center line.

Other automatic operating modes are available with optional equipment. See the last section of this chapter for details.

Plotting Process

Figure 4-5 diagrams the flow of data through the Auto-trol 6035 plotter. The input device chosen by the operator feeds coordinate data into the console for processing up to eight commands per record or card; the console outputs X- and Y-pulse trains to the plotting mechanism at the table.

In drum plotting, Y-pulses go to the head drive to activate a stepping motor that moves the pen back and forth across the paper strip in the Y-direction; X-pulses go to the drum drive to activate a stepping motor that moves the paper strip back and forth under the pen in the X-direction.

The two motions combine to plot the form prescribed by the input data.

In flatbed plotting, X-pulses go to a stepping motor that moves the X-carrier, and Y-pulses go to a stepping motor that moves the Y-head drive. The Y-head holds the pen and therefore moves it in response to the input Y-data; the rails along which the Y-carrier is driven are part of the X-carrier and move with it. Thus, the pen also responds to the input X-data. The pen therefore plots the prescribed form.

Nixie tubes display the X- and Y-coordinates of the point being plotted, a code for the instruction that controls the plot (pen down, dashed line, and so on), and a code for the internal function operating in the controller (stop, delay, and others). A tabulation of the operation and internal function codes (Table 4-10) summarizes the plotting process and the machine-operating cycle. The operation codes mainly initiate the different operating modes. Note that a separate series of codes, 9 through 15, can be used to call for the various operating modes when automatically intermixing drum and flatbed plotting. Operating code 7, calling for a SYMBOL PRINT mode, requires installation of the optional printer. Operation code 8, SELECT mode of operation, is a precedence code signifying that the X-Y pair of codes immediately following it specifies an optional operating mode instead of plot coordinates. For example, an 8 followed by one X-Y pair might command the head to rotate the cutter, and 8 followed by another pair might call for a pen change, and so on. Of course, any optional equipment required by a code sequence must be installed before the sequence is effected.

Table 4-10. Operation Codes

CODE	DRUM CODE	OPERATION
0		No operation
1	9	Move X-Y value
2	10	Pen down; move X-Y value
3	11	SCOOT
4	12	Stop
5	13	Automatic dashed line
6	14	Automatic center line
7	15	Move X-Y value and print symbol
8		Select

As the data processing proceeds, the seven internal function codes appear sequentially in the nixie readout to indicate the portion of the cycle in which the control electronics are operating. First comes a reset portion, then an instruction loading portion, and so forth. A number of indicator lights also help the operator monitor the system.

Software and Options

The manufacturer offers standard plot subroutines written in FORTRAN IV for converting a user's source data into plotter input. The following optional equipment is available for the Auto-trol 6035 plotter:

1. *Printer.* A 62-character alphanumeric mechanical printer with 0 through 9, A through Z, and 26 additional symbols is available. Printing rate is five characters per second, and the entire printer can be rotated 360 degrees for printing at an angle.
2. *Absolute X and Y registers.* This is an option that presents input coordinates in the form of true plus-and-minus absolute values, so that the actual pen position on the table relative to a zero location can be viewed on the nixie display.
3. *Eight-pen turret.* The eight-pen turret allows for automatic selection of eight different pens for varying line widths or colors.
4. *Directional cutter and scribe tool holder.* This is a device for cut-and-peel applications in printed-circuit art work generation and scribing applications in mapping. The tool rotates 360 degrees in 1-degree intervals.
5. *The* CRT *verifying display.* This feature permits verification of drawings for correctness prior to making the finished drawing on the flatbed or drum plotting surface. Plots are drawn on the face of the CRT at a full 50-inch-per-second line speed. After verifying the plot, the data is read in again through the controller and directed to the desired plotting surface. Tube size is 10 inches.
6. *Camera for* CRT. A 35mm camera photographs the pictures drawn on the tube. Film advance and shutter control are fully automatic.

5. FLATBED PLOTTERS AND AUTOMATIC DRAFTING SYSTEMS

INTRODUCTION

Flatbed digital plotters are those in which the plotting medium is rigidly attached to a flat plotting surface; the plot is generated by movements of the plotting head over the fixed surface. Since the plotting medium is not moved back and forth during operation, a wide variety of media can be used—for example, paper, sheet metal, or photographic film. Moreover, as the plotting head is generally in an exposed position above the plotting surface, a wide variety of special-purpose plotting heads and other implements can be attached. For these reasons, flatbed plotters generally have a much greater range of applications than drum plotters; they are also usually more accurate and expensive because of the very rigid construction and close manufacturing tolerances used.

The original application area for flatbed plotters was the production of precise, high-quality drawings on paper or mylar (a drafting medium with high dimensional stability). This area remains an important one; large systems including both plotters and digitizers for the computer production, verification, or modification of engineering working drawings are termed automatic drafting systems and provide much of the market for large flatbed plotters. A digitizer is an important component of a comprehensive automatic drafting system, since it provides the capability of coding drawings for computer processing. In small-scale drafting (that is, with drawings up to about 40 x 60 inches), the digitizer is usually a separate system component. For large-scale operation, it is more economical to use a digitizing attachment on the plotting table (such options are normally available for flatbed plotters with large working surfaces). Digitizing attachments are the subject of Chapter 9.

Plotting media used with flatbed digital plotters include paper, mylar, metal for scribing, photographic film, and various kinds of peelable photographic media; many of these require special plotting tools. Other plotting attachments offered by some manufacturers approach the province of numerically controlled machine tools; examples of these are chemical die cutting, flame cutting, and cloth cutting and sewing for the garment industry. A particularly important application area is the automatic preparation of photographic artwork for use in production of integrated circuits for the electronics industry. One problem here is that plotters operating at the required accuracies are slow, so a rapid means of verifying plot data before photographic plotting is necessary. Cathode-ray tube displays have served this purpose, but their value is limited by their low resolution; establishing hard-copy verification of artwork data is the prime function of the large, fast drum plotters discussed in the preceding chapter.

In addition to large flatbed plotters, a recent innovation is the manufacture of very small, low-cost flatbed plotters for plotting computer output data, usually in connection with time-shared operation. These devices typically have a plotting area no larger than 11 x 7 inches and a small plotting head carrying a single pen. Firms currently offering this type of plotter include Hewlett-Packard, with its HP 7200A, and Gould, with the Brush 1100 plotter.

From this point the chapter concentrates on the larger flatbed plotters, with particular emphasis on the important applications areas of automatic drafting and electronics artwork production. Besides CalComp—which is active in all segments of the digital plotter market, as discussed in Chapter 3—principal suppliers of these flatbed plotting systems are Gerber Scientific, Universal Drafting Machine, Tridea, and Kongsberg. The Gerber Scientific Instrument Company markets a complete range of flatbed plotting systems whose characteristics typify most of the units commonly available; Universal Drafting Machine Corporation and Tridea Electronics are more exclusively aimed at the automatic drafting systems market, while Universal Drafting Machine offers a particularly strong selection of software for the preparation, digitizing, and manipulation of engineering drawings. Kongsberg Systems, Inc., a Norwegian-based company, markets a range of digital plotters and large-scale drafting systems that have made a particularly strong worldwide penetration in the shipbuilding industry.

Most features of available automatic drafting systems are exemplified by the products of the Gerber Scientific Instrument Company, discussed in detail next. CalComp flatbed plotters and drafting systems are included in the general description of CalComp plotters in Chapter 3.

GERBER AUTOMATIC DRAFTING SYSTEMS

General Description

Gerber automatic drafting systems form an integrated product line of precision flatbed digital plotting equipment. The products comprise four plotting system controls and five plotting tables, plus a large number of accessories and options. Any table can connect with any control to form a complete plotting system. Gerber plotting systems are shown in Figures 5-1 and 2-7.

Selection of one of the five flatbed tables for a particular system is made according to the plotting area desired for that system and the system's

Fig. 5-1. Gerber Model 723 automatic drafting system.

Table 5-1. Summary of Gerber Drafting Tables

MODEL	DRAFTING AREA, INCHES	APPLICATION AREAS
22	48 x 58	General-purpose drafting and pattern cutting
23	34 x 44	General-purpose drafting
32	48 x 60	Artwork preparation and high-precision applications
33	24 x 24	Precision photographic artwork; very high precision
75	60 x 96 to 72 x 288	Lofting, large-scale working drawings

application. One class is represented by Models 22 and 23, which are general-purpose digital plotting tables; a second class by Models 32 and 33, which are high-precision tables especially suited to photographic electronics artwork; and a third class by Model 75, a large table useful in such applications as shipbuilding, airframe, and automotive designs. Any of these tables can operate with any of the four system controls (often referred to as drafting machine controls). Pertinent data on the plotting tables appear in Table 5-1; on the controls, in Table 5-2. A notable feature of the Gerber plotting tables is their extremely sturdy construction.

Table 5-2. Summary of Gerber Automatic Drafting Machine Controls

CONTROL	PROGRAM	INPUT	INTERPOLATION	SYMBOL GENERATION	DIGITIZING	VELOCITY OPTIMIZATION
Series 500	Hardwired	On-line computer	Linear	No	No	No
Series 400 and 700	Stored program	Keyboard; paper tape; magnetic tape	Linear; circular	No	No	No
Series 1200	Stored program	Keyboard; paper tape; magnetic tape	Linear; circular*	Yes	Manual	Full look-ahead
Series 2000	Stored program	Keyboard; paper tape; magnetic tape	Linear circular; parabolic†	Yes	Manual, automatic	Full,continuous look-ahead

*Parabolic and cubic interpolation available optionally.
†Cubic interpolation available optionally.

There are five controls: Series 500, Series 400 and 700, Series 1200, and Series 2000, which offer progressively more elaborate capabilities. The Series 400 control is a magnetic-tape version of the Series 700 control, intended primarily for use with the Gerber Model 62 drum plotter mentioned in the preceding chapter. Series 500 is hardwired for on-line computer use of a drafting table; other controls include minicomputers and are intended for off-line plotting from paper or magnetic tape. The earlier Series 600 control (a hardwired control for off-line plotting) and Series 1000 control are now manufactured by Gerber only on special order.

Unlike many digital plotters, the Gerber drafting tables do not employ incremental plotting, which is characterized by a plotting-mechanism rest after each step. By contrast, plotting-head movement in the Gerber systems is smooth and continuous. Pulses sent to the motors in the head-movement mechanisms effect successive accelerations and decelerations that implement the continuous plotting action. Since this method requires sophisticated control, the tables can be used only in conjunction with the Gerber controls.

The standard plotting head is a single-tool device that holds a liquid-ink, fiber-tip, or ball-point pen for drawing applications, or a diamond-scribing implement for cutting. Various optional plotting heads are available, namely, multiple-tool heads, photographic plotting heads, a pattern cutter head (to prepare industrial cardboard patterns), and a cutter simulator head (to simulate the cutter path of a numerically controlled machine tool). A number of digitizing heads are also obtainable, each of which includes a single tool holder.

Options for the tables include positioning aids and roll-feed adapters; options for the controls include magnetic-tape units and other peripheral equipment. Gerber automatic drafting systems can be configured in many ways to suit different applications. Each configuration is designated by a number that joins the plotting table and control model numbers; for example, a Series 700 control and a Model 23 table make up the 723 plotting system. Table 5-3 shows typical systems and indicates the available options and applications for each.

Applications

Gerber automatic drafting systems perform a wide range of industrial applications, depending on the particular table and optional accessories. The Models 22 and 23 tables are most often used for general drafting; Models 32 and 33 tables are mainly used for photographic plotting of electronics artwork; and the Model 75 table is used for preparation of large-scale working drawings.

Table 5-3. Gerber Automatic Drafting Equipment Configurations.

Equipment		System Model	522	523	532	533	575	722	723	732	733
		Control Series	500	500	500	500	500	700	700	700	700
		Table Model	22	23	32	33	75	22	23	32	33
Accessories		Single-Tool Head	*	*	*	*	*	*	*	*	*
		Six-Tool Turret	*	*	*	*	*	*	*	*	*
		Six-Tool In-Line Head									
		Pattern Cutter	*				*	*			
		Cutter Simulator					*				
		Quick Look						*	*	*	*
		Optical Exposure Head	*		*	*	*	*		*	*
		Variable Aperture Photo Exposure Head			*	*				*	*
		TV Camera Head					*				
		Optical Line Follower									
Applications	General Drafting	Diagrams	*	*			*	*	*		
		Architectural	*	*			*	*	*		
		Civil Engineering	*	*			*	*	*		
		Cartography	*	*	*		*	*	*	*	
	Lofting	Shipbuilding					*				
		Automotive					*				
		Aircraft					*				
	Other	Artwork Generation	*	*	*	*		*	*	*	*
		N/C Tape Verification	*	*			*	*	*		
		Manual Digitizing									
		Automatic Digitizing									
		Pattern Generation	*				*	*			

Equipment		System Model	775	1222	1223	1232	1233	1275	2032	2033	2075
		Control Series	700	1200	1200	1200	1200	1200	2000	2000	2000
		Table Model	75	22	23	32	33	75	32	33	75
Accessories		Single-Tool Head	*	*	*	*	*	*	*	*	*
		Six-Tool Turret	*	*	*	*	*		*	*	
		Six-Tool In-Line Head						*			*
		Pattern Cutter	*	*				*			*
		Cutter Simulator	*					*			*
		Quick Look	*	*	*	*	*	*	*	*	*
		Optical Exposure Head		*		*	*	*	*	*	*
		Variable Aperture Photo Exposure Head					*	*	*	*	*
		TV Camera Head				*	*	*	*	*	*
		Optical Line Follower							*	*	*
Applications	General Drafting	Diagrams	*	*	*			*			*
		Architectural	*	*	*			*			*
		Civil Engineering	*	*	*			*			*
		Cartography	*	*	*	*		*	*		*
	Lofting	Shipbuilding	*	*	*			*			*
		Automotive	*					*			*
		Aircraft	*					*			*
	Other	Artwork Generation		*	*	*	*	*	*	*	*
		N/C Tape Verification	*	*	*			*			*
		Manual Digitizing				*	*	*	*	*	*
		Automatic Digitizing							*	*	*
		Pattern Generation	*	*				*			*

There are applications for general drafting on paper, mylar, or vellum in many industries for engineering working drawings, weather maps, architectural drawings, and preparation of masters for the production of business forms. A general requirement in drafting is the production of drawings with repeated subunits such as electronic component symbols or PERT diagram symbols. Gerber provides a general-purpose software package, DRAFT AID, which allows the rapid translation of a rough sketch into a finished drawing or schematic through the use of a graphics input digitizer. In drafting applications where the accuracy of the finished drawing is paramount, working drawings are generally scribed on aluminum, using the scribing tools that Gerber provides for this application.

An important function related to the preparation of engineering drawings is the verification of tapes for numerically controlled machine tools; input tapes for the off-line plotting systems conform to industry standards, and a machine-tool cutter simulator head is available for the Models 22 and 75 tables.

Automatic preparation of electronics artwork is provided by the photographic exposure heads on the Models 32 and 33 tables. Recently, Gerber introduced System 40, a plotting system aimed at the electronics artwork market, which requires very high precision over a small area. (System 40 is discussed separately later in this chapter.) Gerber has developed a software package, the Gerber Graphics Generator (3G) program, that prepares input data for the plotting of electronics artwork, using an IBM/360 computer; output from the 3G program can be used either with System 40 or with other artwork preparation systems that include the Model 32 or Model 33 drafting tables. The Models 32 and 75 tables with the optical exposure head are also being applied to cartography and map making.

Industrial pattern cutting, as for the garment industry, is another area of application. Gerber provides a pattern-cutter head for the Models 22 and 75 tables, which includes a tool holder so that the generated pattern can be annotated. Manual and automatic digitizing equipment is available for many of the Gerber automatic drafting systems.

Input Requirements

Input to a Gerber automatic drafting system depends on the control used and the devices attached to the control. For example, the Series 500 control operates on line to a computer main frame through an interface. Input to the other controls may be obtained from a keyboard, cards, magnetic tape, paper tape, disk, or from a remote computer operating over a communications line.

Input data consists of commands for controlling the plotting tool (e.g., raise/lower pen, select aperture for photographic plotting) and commands for moving the plotting head to generate the plot required. The form of the commands for moving the head depends on the control used. The Series 500 control is a linear interpolator; that is, it accepts commands that specify lines to be drawn. Series 400, Series 700, and Series 1200 controls add circular interpolation, which means that they accept commands for the drawing of circular arcs as well as line segments; parabolic and cubic interpolation are available optionally for the Series 1200 control. Besides the linear and circular capabilities, the Series 2000 control offers parabolic interpolation as a standard feature and cubic interpolation as an optional feature. Series 1200 and Series 2000 controls also accept directives for generating symbols.

Paper-tape and magnetic-tape input to the Series 700, Series 1200, and Series 2000 controls can be accommodated in almost any format by changing the program used for the control's minicomputer. Gerber supports a format that conforms to the EIA (Electronic Industries Association) standard format for input tapes for numerically controlled machine tools, making the firm's drafting systems particularly attractive for the verification of these input tapes prior to use with the actual tools.

Modes of Operation

The control for a Gerber automatic drafting system accepts input from the data device and generates signals to the plotting tool head and pulses to the stepping motors that move the plotting head. The pulses to the stepping motors are generated in such a way that the plotting head produces a series of lines when the Series 500 control is used; a series of lines and circular arcs when the Series 400, 700, or 1200 control is used; or a series of lines, circular arcs, and parabolic arcs when the Series 2000 control is used. When the control is Series 400, 500, or 700, the plotting tool pauses at the end of each arc; however, Series 1200 and Series 2000 controls perform look-ahead and velocity optimization so that this stopping is unnecessary. The velocity optimization performed by the Series 2000 control is more elaborate and efficient than that of the Series 1200 control.

Plotting Process

During plotting, the tool head and the stepping motors controlling its position receive signals from the control to which the table is attached. The signals to the tool head control the selection of the plotting tool, while the pulses to the stepping motors each correspond to one step in distance along the X-axis or the Y-axis. Velocity, acceleration, and deceleration of the plotting head change as the control varies the frequency of the pulses directed to the X and Y stepping motors, so that continuous linear, circular, and parabolic arcs are drawn without a plotting head pause after each step, as is the case with an incremental plotter.

Software

Gerber provides full software support for the Series 400, Series 700, Series 1200, and Series 2000 controls. Besides the software packages available from Gerber, software can be obtained from the manufacturer of the minicomputer included in the control; the control's minicomputer can be put to use as a freestanding computer when the control is not in operation. Series 400, Series 700, and Series 1200 controls include Hewlett-Packard 2114 computers; the Series 2000 control includes a Honeywell H316 computer.

In addition to the software necessary for normal use of the controls, Gerber provides two special-purpose software packages: DRAFT AID for the Series 1200 control and the Gerber Graphics Generator (3G) program, a FORTRAN program for generation of electronics artwork data tapes on an IBM/360 computer. Further applications software is under development.

DRAFT AID. This special package is used in preparing accurate drawings from rough sketches. It was originally developed for use with the Series 1200 control and the Model 23 drafting table, but any of the drafting tables can be used. A cassette-tape unit and a card reader must be added to the Series 1200 control to adapt it for DRAFT AID. Input to DRAFT AID, taken either from a Teletypewriter keyboard or from a paper-tape reader, consists of a series of DRAFT AID language statements that describe the required drawing. Standard subdrawings, such as electronic components, may be called from a library stored on a cassette tape.

Gerber has announced an enhanced version of DRAFT AID. With this revised package, data for the drawing to be generated is input from the GCD-1 large area coordinate digitizer. Since all current users of DRAFT AID systems have GCD-1 digitizers, this version supersedes the previous DRAFT AID software package. The DRAFT AID language is now used only to specify symbols for inclusion in the cassette magnetic-tape library.

Applications of DRAFT AID include logic diagrams; electrical, electronic, and piping schematics; architectural layouts; and PERT charts. Figure 5-2 shows a typical drawing generated with the DRAFT AID package in ink on mylar; it took about 1 hour of digitizing time and 17 minutes of plotting time, compared with an estimated 7 hours for equivalent manual drafting.

GERBER GRAPHICS GENERATOR (3G). The 3G program generates input data tapes for photographic plotting of electronics artwork. It was initially

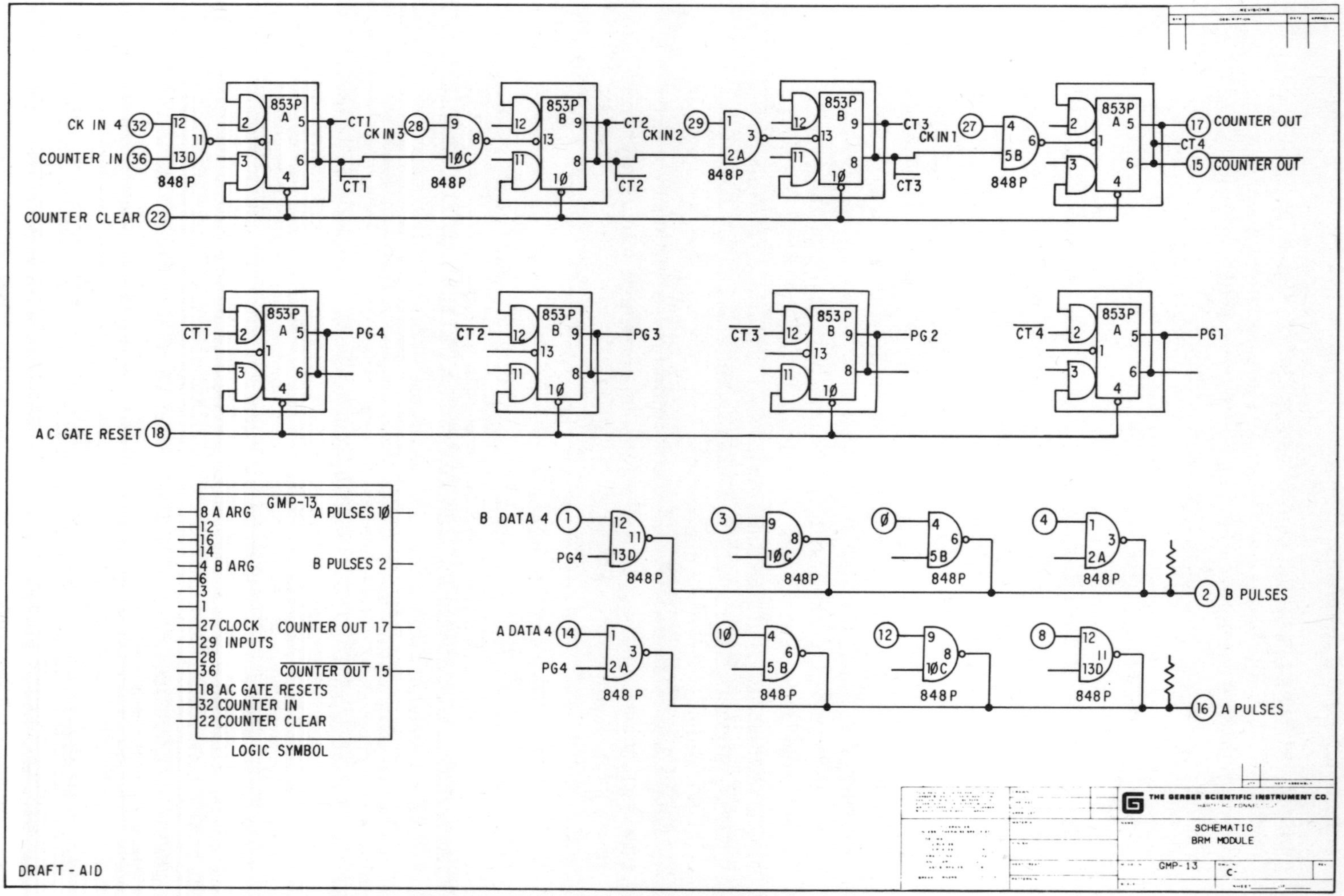

Fig. 5-2. Typical drawing produced with the Draft Aid software package.
(Reprinted with permission of the Gerber Scientific Instrument Co.)

designed for use on the Gerber System 40, but can also be used in conjunction with photographic plotting equipment on the Model 32 or Model 33 drafting table. The 3G is coded in FORTRAN and assembly language for an IBM/360 computer. It can be run on any computer compatible with an IBM/360 Model 30 that has at least 65, 536 bytes of core storage, a card reader, disk, and a suitable output device. The 3G program-generation artwork input data for circuits is specified by the 3G input language, which is a high-level, special-purpose specification language that furnishes such facilities as the repetition of subpatterns and the filling in of polygonal areas.

Options

Options for the Gerber automatic drafting systems are of three types: tool heads, digitizing heads, and drafting table accessories. A complete listing of the options and the tables with which they are available appears in Table 5-4. Besides these options, a number of other features, such as additional peripheral devices and main memory, are available for the controls.

Optional tool heads provide capabilities for the use of multiple or special-purpose drafting tools. The dual-, three-, and six-tool heads simply hold a number of pens or scribing implements that can be selected under program or operator control when a number of tools are needed for a single plot. There are two different types of multitool heads: turret heads and the six-tool in-line head. The turret heads, which do not require any offset when the selected tool is changed, were developed for use with hardwired controls; the six-tool in-line head was developed for use with the Series 2000 control, which can provide the necessary tool offsets by program.

The *pattern-cutting head*, used for the cutting and annotation of industrial patterns, is equipped with a marking tool and a knife whose rotation is under program control. The *cutter simulator head* contains a rotating stylus to simulate the path of a numerically controlled machine tool on pressure-sensitive paper and includes a marking tool for annotating the plot and marking the centerline of the cutter. The *rotatable knife head* includes a bidirectional knife whose rotation is under program control; it is used for peeling Peel Coat material—a laminated mylar photographic material used, for example, in the preparation of integrated-circuit masks and comparator charts.

Characteristics of the *photographic plotting heads* available are summarized in Table 5-5. There are two types, fixed aperture and variable aperture; between them, they are capable of meeting all the plotting requirements of the different types of electronics artwork currently produced. The heads include a tool holder for nonphotographic plotting. Both head types can be mounted together on the Model 32 or the Model 33 drafting tables. Photographic plotting takes place on materials up to 0.25 inch thick; master negatives are usually created on glass.

There are two different models of the fixed-aperture photographic head, depending on the table to be used. These heads include a turret containing masks for 24 different apertures; an aperture can be selected under operator or program control, and custom-design apertures may be speci-

Table 5-4. Optional Accessories Available for Gerber Drafting Tables

TABLE	MODEL 22	MODEL 23	MODEL 32	MODEL 33	MODEL 75
Tool heads*					
Dual tool head	x	x			
3-position tool holder	x	x			
6-tool turret	x	x	x	x	x
6-tool in-line head					x
Pattern-cutter head	x				x
Cutter simulator head					x
Rotatable knife head		x	x		
Photo-optical exposure heads					
Model OEH-1	x	x			
Model OEH-B			x	x	x
Variable-aperture photo exposure head			x	x	
Step-and-repeat head			x	x	
Digitizing heads*†					
TV camera head, with or without single tool†			x	x	x
TV zoom lens head, 2 tools†					x
Automatic line follower‡					x
Quick Look§	x	x	x	x	x
Other accessories					
Absolute reference point			x	x	
Manual gear change			x		
Manual roll feed	x				x
Optical magnifier	x	x	x	x	x
Reversible vacuum					x
Metric gearing					x
Slew controls					x

*A tool head must be purchased with each table.
†Manual digitizing requires a Series 1200 or Series 2000 control.
‡Automatic digitizing requires a Series 2000 control.
§Quick Look requires a Series 400, Series 700, Series 1200, or Series 2000 control.

Table 5-5. Characteristics of Gerber Photographic Plotting Heads

DATA	FIXED-APERTURE PHOTOGRAPHIC MODELS OEH-1	OEH-B	VARIABLE-APERTURE PHOTOGRAPHIC, MODEL VAPE II
Applicable drafting tables	22, 23	32,33, 75	32,33
Apertures	24 fixed, program-selectable		1 fixed, changeable by operator; 1 variable, program-selectable, rectangular
Aperture sizes, inches	0.002 x 0.002 to 0.187 x 0.187	0.005 x 0.005 to 0.240 x 0.240	Fixed: up to 1.5 x 1.5 Variable: 0.006 x 0.006 to 2.000 x 2.000 in steps of 0.001
Mechanical specifications			Accuracy ±0.002 inch Repeatability ±0.0005 inch Squareness ±1 minute
Image tolerances	Normal speeds: 0.002–0.005 inch ±0.0003 inch 0.006–0.150 inch ±0.0005 inch 0.151–0.187 inch ±0.001 inch Intermediate speeds: 0.004–0.005 inch ±0.0005 inch 0.006–0.150 inch ±0.0007 inch 0.151–0.187 inch ±0.001 inch	0.007–0.015 inch ±0.0005 inch 0.016–0.050 inch ±0.001 inch 0.051–0.100 inch ±0.002 inch 0.101–0.240 inch ±0.003 inch	
Turret indexing (at film plane)	Relocation of same aperture ±0.0001 inch Maximum positional error between different apertures ±0.0006 inch	Relocation of same aperture ±0.0003 inch Maximum positional error between different apertures ±0.001 inch	
Maximum axial plotting speed	Model 32 table 60-150 inches/min; Model 33 table 60 inches/min	150 inches/min	

fied. The entire turret assembly or individual apertures can be changed by the operator. The heads operate in two modes: flash or line drawing. In flash mode, the aperture pattern simply flashes onto the film beneath the head without head movement; in line-drawing operation the head moves over the plotting surface with the shutter open. There is a variable-density filter over the light source, which connects via a servomechanism to sensors for the plotting speed, so that the film exposed in line-drawing mode receives constant exposure as the plotting speed changes.

The variable-aperture photographic head is similar to the fixed-aperture head except that it has one fixed aperture and one variable aperture, the latter being a rectangle whose dimensions can be changed by the program. The fixed aperture can be changed by the operator in a few minutes. Motors that change the aperture size operate incrementally. The variable aperture must be fully opened for use of the one fixed aperture. Like the fixed-aperture photographic head, the variable-aperture head provides for constant exposure of the film at different aperture sizes and plotting speeds; it is also equipped with an interlock to stop plotting in the case of bulb failure.

To reduce the production time for photographic plots containing repeated information, Gerber has introduced the step-and-repeat head, which can be used with the OEH and/or VAPE heads on a Model 32 or Model 33 drafting table. The head uses a photographic master plate up to 10 x 12 inches, to produce an image up to 9 x 11 inches on the plotting medium. When using the step-and-repeat head, it is first positioned over the point to be exposed. Then the master plate is lowered and vacuum-sealed against the plotting surface during the flash exposure. The process

Table 5-6. Quick Look Specifications

CHARACTERISTIC	DESCRIPTION
Display size	
Vertical	6-7/16 inches
Horizontal	8-5/32 inches
Display tube	Flat face, storage
Display resolution	
Horizontal	400 line pairs
Vertical	300 line pairs
Viewing time	
Recommended	15 min, regularly
Permissible	1 hr, when required
Physical	
Overall dimensions	22 inches long by 11 inches wide by 17 inches high
Weight	60 lb

of lowering the plate, flashing an exposure, and raising the head takes 10 seconds; positioning accuracy and repeatability tolerances do not exceed those of the table on which the head is being used by more than 0.0002 inch.

Usually, the entire master plate is exposed at each flash of the step-and-repeat head; however, the photocomposition option for the head can be used to prepare master plates consisting of a number of standard patterns, which can be selected and flashed separately. The appropriate offset of the head is achieved by control electronics. Since use of the step-and-repeat head does not interfere with operation of either the VAPE or OEH head, different photographic heads can be combined for a single photographic plot.

Digitizing equipment available for the Gerber plotting tables is more fully described in Chapter 9 on digitizers and automatic drafting machines. Options available include a digitizing TV head, which includes a closed-circuit TV camera for viewing of graphic data during digitizing, and the automatic line follower for automatic conversion of graphical data to digital form.

The *Quick Look* device is a cathode-ray tube display that allows a rapid inspection of plotting data; its main application is the checking of photographic plot data. The required software support means that this accessory is available only with the Series 1200 and Series 2000 controls. A windowing feature enables any selected portion of the display to be enlarged to the full size of the screen. See Table 5-6 for full specifications of Quick Look.

Available *drafting table accessories* include optical magnifiers for precise positioning of plotting heads over existing drawings, an absolute reference point feature for exact registration of different parts of multilayer artwork and roll-feed features. The manual gear-change feature on the Model 32 table allows operator selection of plotting speed and accuracy. The reversible vacuum feature available for the Model 75 table is used to aid the placement of drafting plates on the table—the plates are "floated" onto the table on a cushion of air. (Refer to Table 5-4 for a complete listing of the available accessories.)

GERBER SYSTEM 40

General Description

The Gerber System 40 automatic artwork generator (Fig. 5-3) is a special-purpose, self-contained digital plotting system intended primarily for the automatic generation of printed-circuit artwork masters. It is designed for photographic plotting; however, a single-tool holder allows plotting by pen or scribing instrument on mylar, vellum, or other standard drafting media.

Fig. 5-3. Gerber System 40 automatic artwork generator.

Input data is taken from paper tape, magnetic tape, or punched cards. It is generated either by digitizing a graphical design or by a computer program, using software supplied by Gerber. A vacuum holds the plotting medium on a rubber platen, which is attached to a moving platform beneath the fixed plotting head. Output generally consists of finished, full-size artwork masters for direct use in printed-circuit production, with no further photographic processes required. Photosensitive materials up to 0.25 inch thick can be used.

Although developed and initially marketed as a separate product, the System 40 and control can be configured with the other Gerber plotting tables and controls. Other artwork generation systems manufactured by Gerber are all part of its standard, integrated product line. These systems, which use Models 32 and 33 plotting tables, are more expensive than System 40, but offer the advantages of greater accuracy and larger plotting areas.

Applications

System 40 is primarily for photographic plotting, but can also be used for general drafting by pen or scribing implement using the single-tool head, which is included. Photographic applications include the preparation of printed-circuit artwork, integrated-circuit masks, and engineering comparator charts. These charts are precise photographic images of precision components that are projected for comparison and reference during the machining of the part. Typical applications are in the production of precision gear teeth and jet-engine vanes.

Input Requirements

System 40 input consists of variable-length command blocks coded in accordance with the standards for numerically controlled machine tools set by the Electronic Industry Association. Each block of information may include incremental X- and Y-coordinates for a plotting movement and a command as follows:

1. X-dimension for next step.*
2. Y-dimension for next step.*
3. Pen down or shutter open.
4. Pen up or shutter closed.
5. Flash.
6. Selected specified aperture (1 of 24).

Table 5-7. Gerber System 40 Input Devices

INPUT MEDIUM	RATED SPEED	DEVICE
Punched card	14 col/sec	User-supplied IBM 029 reader
Punched tape	300 char./sec	Gerber paper-tape reader
Magnetic tape		
7-track; 200/556/800 bits/inch	6,000-24,000 char./sec	Gerber MT12-7 buffered magnetic-tape reader
9-track, 800 bits/inch	24,000 char./sec	Gerber MT12-9 buffered magnetic-tape reader
Teletypewriter	10 char./sec	Teletype ASR 33

Input data can be taken from paper tape, punched cards, magnetic tape, or a Teletypewriter keyboard, using the input devices noted in Table 5-7.

Modes of Operation and Operator Controls

Input commands are converted by the hardwired controller into a series of incremental commands to the plotting table and plotting head. Each

*X- and Y-dimensions for the next step each consist of four decimal digits plus sign, giving a range of ± 9.999.

pulse to the X or Y stepping motor moves the carriage 0.0005 inch.

Commands for the plotting head also control the plot. When a tool is being used, only pen down/pen up commands are applicable, but more extensive commands are available for photographic plotting. These comprise commands to open or close the shutter, to select one of the 24 apertures on the head, and to trigger FLASH mode operation. The FLASH mode operation exposes a standard aperture pattern on the film below the head; the normal line-drawing mode, on the other hand, exposes a line by causing the film to move below the open shutter. In the line-drawing modes, the speed of movement varies according to the selected aperture size, to maintain a constant film exposure.

Operator controls for System 40 include buttons for activating the plotting head and the vacuum holddown. Mirror-image switches for the X- and Y-axes allow selection of the positive direction of motion along either axis.

Plotting Process

During plotting, the hardwired controller controls the reading of the input data and converts the input commands (listed under "Input Requirements") into directives to the plotting heads and the positioning step motors. A major feature of the controller is the facility to draw a line from the current position of the table under the head to any specified point by generating the series of plotting motor steps needed. This capability, known as linear interpolation, is a standard feature of many automatic drafting machines and numerically controlled machine tools.

Software

No software is necessary for System 40 itself, since the controller is hardwired and the system operates off line only. However, a software package is available for the preparation of input data on a computer rather than by manual digitizing. This package, called the 3G (Gerber Graphics Generator) program, is coded in FORTRAN and assembly language for an IBM/360 computer. It can be run on any computer compatible with an IBM/360 Model 30 that has at least 65,536 bytes of core storage, a card reader, disk, and a suitable output device. The 3G program-generation artwork input data for circuits is specified by the 3G input language, a high-level, special-purpose, specification language that furnishes such facilities as the repetition of subpatterns and the filling in of polygonal areas. Figure 5-4 shows an example of printed-circuit artwork plotted by System 40 with input data generated by the 3G program.

Output from the 3G program can also be used to produce artwork on other Gerber artwork generation systems.

Options

Optional features for System 40 include a lightproof hood for use in an environment with normal artificial lighting and a lightproof enclosure for daylight operation. A metric version of System 40 is also available.

When producing printed-circuit artwork for multilayer applications (Fig. 5-4), it is important to maintain accurate registration between different pieces of artwork for the same assembly. For this purpose an absolute reference-point feature fixes an accurate origin for a plot, and special positioning pins are inserted in the plotting surface to help place the drafting medium.

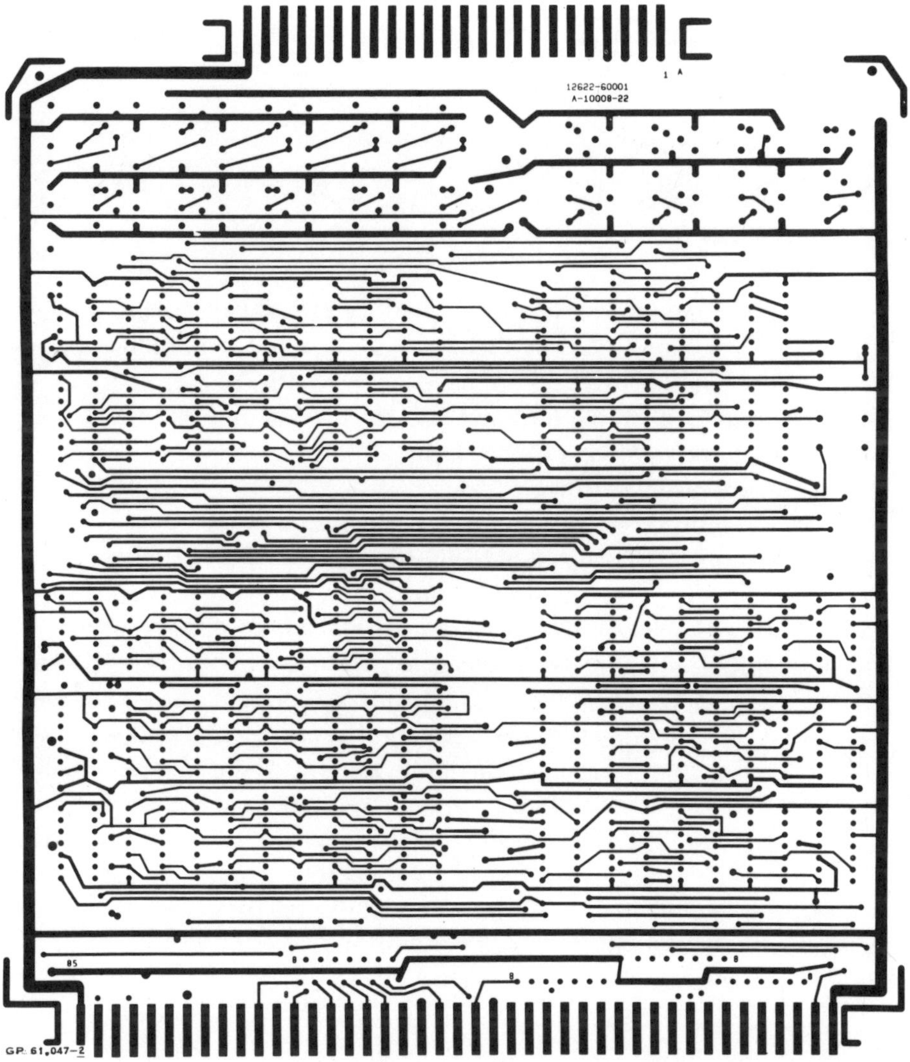

Fig. 5-4. This is the component slide of a double-sided printed-circuit board. It was plotted on a Gerber System 40 artwork generator in 25 minutes.

6. OTHER PLOTTING TECHNOLOGIES

INTRODUCTION

Besides the conventional digital plotters already discussed, devices with radically different plotting technologies have been offered by a number of other manufacturers who have entered the plotter market. An example is provided by the Xynetics automated drafting systems, a series of flatbed plotters in which a free-running plotting head is moved magnetically over the plotting surface.

Other examples are the GeoSpace Corporation plotters, which use a cathode-ray-tube (CRT) projection technique; the recently announced Gerber Model 82 electrographic plotter, plotting on specially prepared sheets of paper using a stylus and a toner; and the Dresser LGP 2000 plotter, producing photographic plots by means of a pulsed laser beam. Digital plots can also be generated using nonimpact printers, CRT displays, or computer-output microfilm devices, which are beyond the scope of this book.

Many of the new types of plotters have generated considerable technical interest, their ultimate place in the market being naturally dependent on the particular applications for which they are most suitable. This chapter illustrates the diversity of plotter technologies by including detailed discussions of two unconventional digital plotting systems—the Xynetics automated drafting systems and the Dresser LGP 2000 Lasergraphic® plotter.*

*The name Lasergraphic® is a registered trademark of Dresser Systems, Inc.

XYNETICS AUTOMATED DRAFTING SYSTEMS

General Description

The Xynetics automated drafting systems consist of a family of three flatbed digital drafting tables with associated controls, interfaces, and options for on-line or off-line plotting in a variety of different applications. They are of particular technical interest because they operate on an unconventional basis (named the Sawyer principle, for its inventor). Specifically, the plotting tool is held in a free-running head supported on an air bearing and moved by the interaction of electromagnets and a fixed grid of magnetic material. Available plotting tools include pens, scribes, cutters, thermochromic plotting tools, and a photographic plotting head.

Xynetics plotters are fast compared to more conventional flatbed plotters, because of the low inertia of the plotting head. While their accuracy, repeatability, and resolution are consistent with the requirements of general engineering drafting and most cartographic activities, they do not match the high accuracies of flatbed plotters intended largely for integrated-circuit electronics artwork generation.

Fig. 6-1. Plotting head of Xynetics 1100 automated drafting system.

Characteristics of the Xynetics plotting tables are given in Table 6-1, and Table 6-2 presents characteristics of the C60 Series controls. Figure 6-1 shows the plotting head of a Xynetics 1100 automated drafting system; a view of a complete system is included in Chapter 2.

Applications

The Xynetics automated drafting systems are generally satisfactory for flatbed digital plotting applications except for those that require extreme accuracy. Plotting may be by liquid-ink, felt-tip, or ball-point pen, scribing and cutting tools, or thermochromic plotting tools. Photographic plotting heads are among the optional tools available; photographic materials up to ¼ inch thick can be accommodated, permitting the creation of glass master negatives for electronics artwork preparation. Other applications areas cited by Xynetics include architectural, automotive, cartographic, seismic, shipbuilding, and roadbuilding applications.

Applications areas for which Xynetics provides software packages include computer program flow charting, contouring, and verification of tapes for numerically controlled machine tools. Software routines are available for the programming of business, scientific, and drafting applications, as well as for basic and general plotting applications.

Input Requirements

Input to a Xynetics automated drafting system is obtained from a com-

Table 6-1. Characteristics of Xynetics Plotting Tables

TABLE	500	1100	1200
Work area, inches	25 x 42 (max. sheet size, 48 x 64)	42 x 57 (max. sheet size, 48 x 64)	57 x 89 (max. sheet size, 64 x 96)
Positional accuracy, inches	0.005 over whole area; 0.001 over 1 sq. ft		
Repeatability, inches	0.001		
Max. speed, inches/min	2400 (400 with software slope generator)		
Drive mechanism	Sawyer principle electromagnetic drive; see text		
Work-surface orientation	Fixed horizontal		
Vacuum holddown	Optional	Standard	Standard
Types of plotting	Liquid-ink, ball-point, or felt-tip pen; scribe; thermochromic; photographic		

Table 6-2. Characteristics of C60 Series Controls

MODEL	INPUT	MAIN MEMORY SIZE, 16-BIT WORDS
C60	Magnetic tape, 9-track, 800 bpi or 7-track 556/800 bpi, 25 inches/sec	4096
C61	Paper tape, 400 char/sec	4096
C62	Magnetic tape, 9-track, 800 bpi or 7-track, 556/800 bpi, 25 inches/sec	8192
C63	Paper tape, 400 char/sec	8192

puter in on-line operation or from paper or magnetic tape in off-line operation. All systems employ a controller, which includes a minicomputer and a Teletypewriter. Software for the controller is provided by Xynetics; with this system, the minicomputer can also be operated separately, particularly for the preparation of plotting data using software FORTRAN routines provided by Xynetics. Plotting software is described in a later section.

Configurations for operation of the modular plotting systems, which incorporate the 500, 1100, and 1200 drafting tables, are shown in Figure 6-2; the components of these systems are discussed in the following paragraphs.

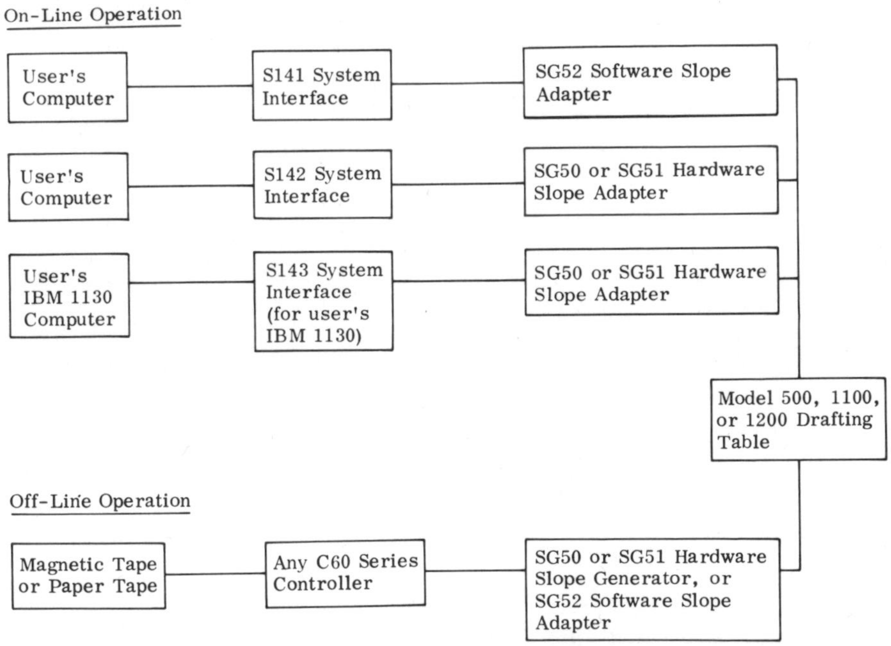

Fig. 6-2. Configuration for Xynetics automated drafting systems.

SYSTEM INTERFACES. These interfaces are needed to connect a user's computer output channel to a slope generator and thence to a drafting table for on-line operation. The S141 interface is used with the software slope adapter; there are two interfaces for use with the hardware slope generators—the general-purpose S142 interface, and the special-purpose S143 interface for use with an IBM 1130 computer.

CONTROLLERS. Characteristics of the C60 Series of plotting controllers are summarized in Table 6-2. Xynetics provides two sets of controlling software: a basic version, for a main memory of 4096 words; and an enhanced version, for a controller having at least 8192 words of computer main memory. The basic controller software package features input data buffering, internal control of the velocity and acceleration of the plotting head, and facilities for searching tape-plotting data files. Software for controllers with at least 8192 words of main memory provides alphanumeric character generation and expanded operator controls in the enhanced version.

SLOPE GENERATOR. The system interface (for on-line plotting) or C60 Series controller (for off-line plotting) must connect to the drafting table via a slope generator, as shown in Figure 6-2. The slope generator interpolates; i.e., it accepts commands to the plotting head to execute a drawing. There are three types of slope generators: the SG52 software slope adapter, which enables the functions of the slope generator to be performed by controlling software; the SG50 hardware slope generator, which is a linear interpolator; and the SG51 hardware arc/slope generator, which is a linear and circular interpolator. The hardware slope generators are more expensive than the software slope adapter, but are necessary to attain the full plotting speed; the maximum plotting speed of 40 inches per second is reduced to about 15 inches per second when the software slope adapter is used.

Modes of Operation

The Xynetics drafting tables have a single mode of operation in which signals from the slope generator to the plotting head cause head movement through interaction of the electromagnets in the plotting head with a fixed matrix of magnetic material. Movement of the plotting head is smooth and continuous; the head does not stop moving between successive commands as in an incremental plotter. Because of the different degrees of sophistication of the interpolation performed by the slope generators, the plotting head movement is in a series of straight-line segments when the software slope adapter or the hardware slope generator is used.

Under the control of the hardware arc/slope generator, however, movement of the head consists of a series of line segments and circular arcs. The

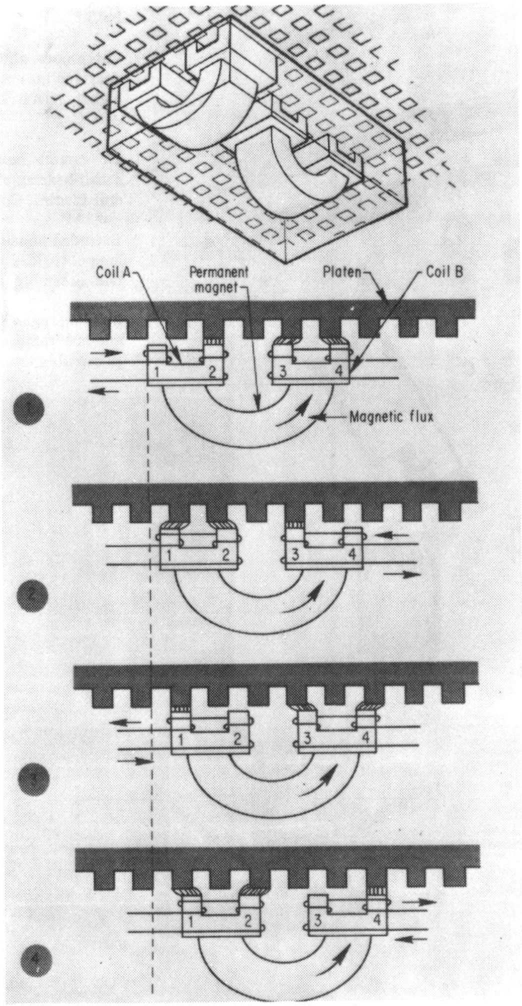

Fig. 6-3. Sawyer principle of operation (simplified diagrams). Top: typical arrangement of magnets in actual plotting head. Numbers 1 through 4 indicate motion of head from right to left produced by pulsing of electromagnets.

hardware arc/slope generator includes a velocity optimization feature that allows plotting to proceed from one line or arc to the next without the plotting head coming to rest unnecessarily.

Plotting Process

During plotting, the plotting head is supported on an air bearing maintained by a stream of air piped to it from a fractional horsepower pump, and pulses directed to electromagnets in the head interact with a fixed matrix of magnetic material to produce head movement. This process is shown in Figure 6-3; the fixed magnetic matrix consists of a waffle-pattern array of squares of magnetic material embedded in an epoxy matrix above the plotting surface and head. Although the matrix of squares is on 40-mil centers, the stepping pulses provided for the electromagnets give a resolution of 1 mil.

The maximum stepping rate is 30,000 steps per second along either axis, giving a maximum plotting speed of 30 inches per second axially, which is equivalent to a maximum diagonal plotting speed of about 40 inches per second. Stepping action means that the electromagnets must be pulsed for every 1-mil movement along either axis, but the plotting head does not come to rest after each step. Its speed and direction of motion are controlled by the frequencies of the stepping signals from the slope generator.

Software

Besides the controlling software for the C60 Series, Xynetics provides three levels of software for preparation of plotting data for its automated drafting system: (1) basic software; (2) functional software; (3) applications software. All Xynetics software is written in FORTRAN, for compatibility with a large number of different computers, and is supplied free of charge with the purchase or lease of a Xynetics drafting table.

Basic Software

The basic software consists of an integrated set of plotting subroutines that prescribe basic plotting operations. Subroutines are available for initializing a plot, selecting a pen, and locating the plotting head. Other subroutines generate lines, circular arcs, axes, and alphanumeric characters.

In addition, subroutine capabilities include automatic incorporation of scaling and offset factors in the plot being generated, and communication with the operator via the Teletypewriter. Subroutines in the basic software package are summarized in Table 6-3.

Table 6-3. Xynetics Basic Software

SUBROUTINE	FUNCTION
DIMTAB	Initialization routine
PLOT	Generates movement of pen
SYMBOL	Creates character annotation
ARC	Generates circular arcs
WHERE	Gives the position of pen
FACTOR	Issues new scale factor
SCALE	Determines scales and offsets
LINE	Generates lines and/or symbols
NUMBER	Creates numeric annotation
AXIS	Generates axis, annotation, labels and tic marks
OFFSET	Sets offset parameters
MESAGE	Communication with TTY
PEN	Changes pens mounted on plotter head

Functional Software

Xynetics functional software comprises a set of FORTRAN routines that have general application in particular fields but are of a higher level than the set of basic software subroutines. Functional software is divided into the areas of general, drafting, scientific, and business applications. The subroutines provided in the functional software package are summarized in Table 6-4.

Table 6-4. Xynetics Functional Software

APPLICATION AREA	SUBROUTINE	FUNCTION
General	DASHLN	Draws dashed lines connecting a series of datum points
	CIRCAL	Draws a circle or arc through three points
	ELLIPS	Draws an ellipse or elliptical arc
	GRID	Draws a linear grid
	POLY	Draws an equilateral polygon
	SPIRAL	Draws a spiral arc
Drafting	AROWHD	Draws arrowheads
	CNTRL	Draws a centerline
Business	AXISCA	Draws an axis with calendar-month annotation
	BAR	Draws bars for bar graphs
	SHADE	Shades specified polygonal area
Scientific	CURVX	Plots a polynomial function of X over a given range
	CURVY	Plots a polynomial function of Y over a given range

Applications Software

The applications software consists of complete FORTRAN programs for particular applications. Three applications programs are currently available for contouring, flow chart generation, and tape verification for numerically controlled machine tools.

XYCP. (Xynetics Contouring Program). The XYCP is a generalized surface approximation, that contours and plots a program for three-dimensional data. Applications areas include geophysics, meteorology, engineering, electrical and magnetic field intensities, and biological and medical applications.

FLOW GRAM. This plotting software program generates a flow chart for any standard FORTRAN program. Output from the program is formatted on 8½ x 11-inch pages for ease of storage.

APT. This plotting software package provides a graphical representation of control tape for numerically controlled machine tools, for checking purposes. It provides a plot of the cutter path; scaling of the generated plot can be adjusted to match that of the blueprint so that the path can be easily checked against a drawing of the part to be machined.

Options

Options for the plotting tables themselves include a vacuum holddown feature for the Model 500 table (this feature is standard on the other tables) and an axis-position display feature, which provides an illuminated display of the current position of the plotting head. The slope generators and other options connected with the way the system operates were discussed above.

Standard equipment for each table includes a four-pen tool holder, one plotting pen, and actuators for liquid-ink, felt-tip, or ball-point pens. Optional plotting accessories for use with the standard plotting head include: the *four-pen kit,* which includes three additional pen actuators, assorted liquid-ink, felt-tip, and ball-point pens; and an ultrasonic cleaner; the *scribe kit,* which contains a scribing adapter and a diamond scribe for use on scribe-coat material or painted-plate media; and the *thermochromic pen kit,* which has four pens with individual force and current control, for plotting on thermosensitive media.

Photographic plotting capabilities are provided by the *photo head.* This device includes a Xenon lamp, which is flashed through a shaped aperture to produce an image on the plotting surface. Photographic plotting speeds of 10, 5, or 3 inches per second are attainable, depending on the photographic plotting medium in use. The photographic plotting head cannot be used with the SG52 software slope adapter; one of the hardware slope generators must be used.

The aperture that shapes the flashed image is program-selectable from an assortment on an aperture wheel included in the photohead. The standard wheel provides 18 different apertures, consisting of round, square, pad, and fiducial mark patterns; for this standard aperture wheel an accuracy of 0.001 inch and a repeatability of 0.0005 inch are quoted. Aperture wheels can be supplied to customer specifications, the number of different apertures on a customer-specified aperture wheel depending on the design of the particular wheel. The length and width of any aperture lie between 0.003 and 0.250 inch.

DRESSER LGP 2000 LASERGRAPHIC PLOTTER

General Description

The Dresser LGP 2000 lasergraphic plotter employs a laser beam that scans photographic film line by line to expose a succession of connected dots that form the desired plot in a manner analogous to picture formation on a TV screen. The dots are exposed under the control of the host computer and in accordance with the data it provides.

Upon completion of a row, the film is advanced one line while the beam is returned to the starting position. This cycle is repeated and continued until the entire length of film has been exposed. The resulting image is

Fig. 6-4. LGP 2703 plotter and associated components.

contained within a 40 inch wide strip centered in 42-inch roll film 100 feet long.

Two plotting resolutions are possible, namely, 5 mils (200 dots per inch) and 10 mils (100 dots per inch). Each installation can be preset at the factory for any three selectable plotting rates corresponding to film speeds of up to 19 inches per second for 10-mil resolution and up to 9.5 inches per second for 5-mil resolution. The user, of course, specifies rates that are compatible with the data transfer rate of the computer channel to be attached to the plotter.

The film is both advanced and cut under computer control. Film processing, which must take place in complete darkness, is performed by automatic equipment available for the purpose.

The LGP-2703 plotter is shown in Figure 6-4, between the magnetic-tape unit on the far side and the Raytheon 703 computer in the foreground. For each computer to be operated with the plotting system, suitable interfacing circuits must be added to the basic plotter. Model numbers are assigned accordingly, as indicated in Table 6-5.

Table 6-5. Plotter-Computer Pairs in Off-Line Operation

PLOTTER MODEL	COMPUTER
LGP 2000	IBM/360, Model 25 and larger models
LGP 2180	IBM 1800
LGP 2703	Raytheon 703
LGP 2706	Raytheon 706

Note: Interfaces for other computers can be supplied upon request.

INTERPRETATION. Utilization of a pulsed laser-energy source enables the LGP-2000 to achieve high data-transfer rates. In addition, recording on long roll film provides the capacity for extremely long continuous plots, a necessity in the seismic applications for which the LGP-2000 was originally developed. Duplicates can be readily generated from the master film. The unusual ability to plot in shades of gray is especially suited for pictorial applications such as the plotting of information received from spacecraft. In this application field a 1-mil resolution is frequently preferred to the 5-mil limit of the LGP-2000, but this limitation is often offset by the ability to execute much larger plots than those of most competitive devices.

It must be recognized that the LGP-2000 scanning sequence necessitates the creation of large amounts of data. The software routines supplied by Dresser definitely simplify the problems of programming; but, of course, the user must be prepared to incorporate Dresser routines into his own existing programs. He must also install facilities for processing the film.

Modes of Operation

An LGP-2000 plotter system in on-line operation consists of a computer controlled by both user and manufacturer software, a computer data channel built into the computer or an alternative interface, and the plotter itself. Since the plot is drawn on roll film, no plotting table is employed. On-line operation is represented in the upper part of Figure 6-5.

In so-called off-line operation, an LGP-2000 system consists of data tape generated by the host computer, a magnetic-tape transport, a medium-size computer to perform reformatting, an interface, and the plotter. It follows that the plotter operates off line only with respect to the host computer. The lower part of Figure 6-5 presents the basic configuration of this operating mode. Table 6-5 is a partial list of possible plotter-computer combinations.

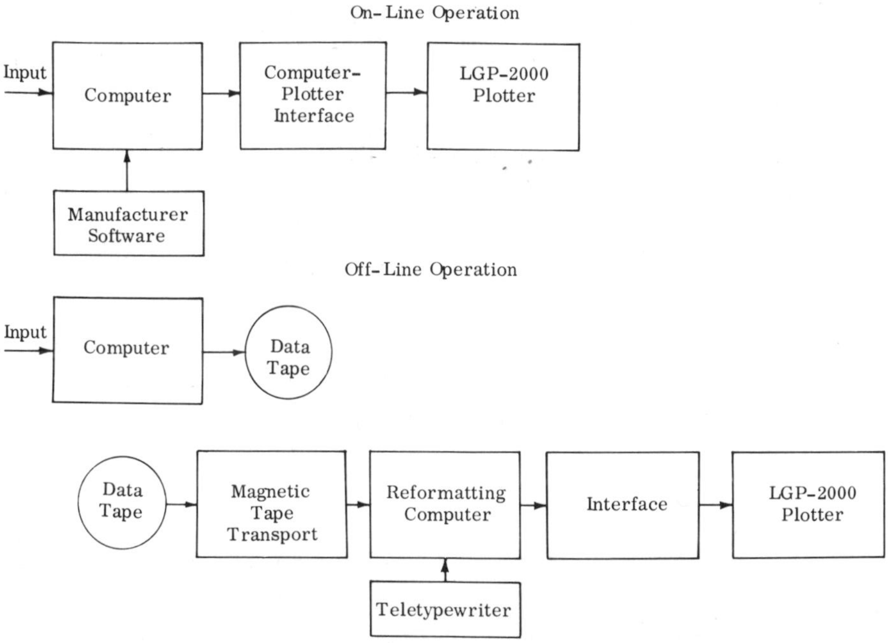

Fig. 6-5. Block diagram of LGP-2000 plotter system on-line and off-line operation.

The LGP-2000 is shown schematically in Figure 6-6. It consists of the following main components:

1. Laser source and control system.
2. Rotating mirror/command synchronizer assembly.
3. Film transport and stepping logic.
4. Interface electronics.

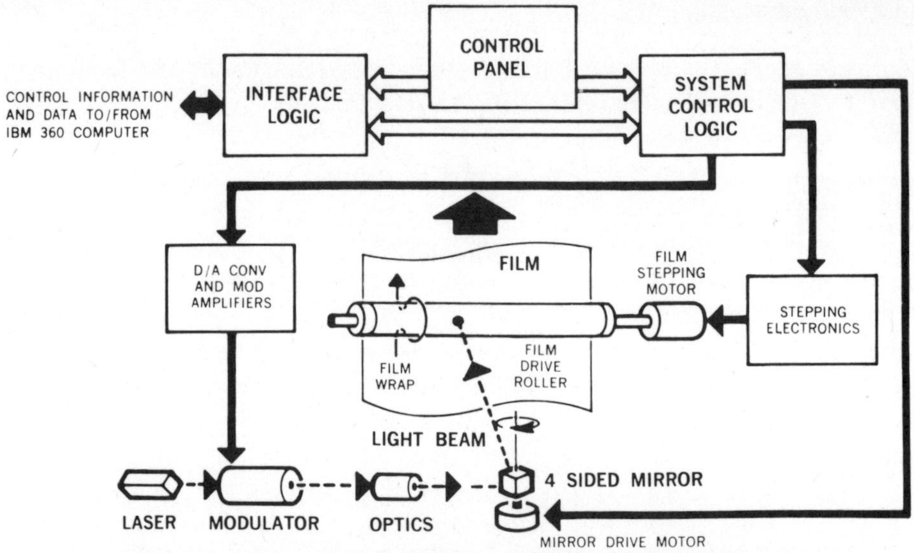

Fig. 6-6. Block diagram of the LGP 2000 Lasergraphic plotter.

Input signals, consisting of both plotting data and control information, are taken from the controlling computer. Data transfer to the plotter is enhanced by two buffer registers in the LGP 2000, which store data received from the computer while plotting takes place. Light from a laser source is modulated in accordance with the input data and then deflected left to right by a rotating mirror. The laser is pulsed to expose a sequence of points across the film. When one row of points has been exposed, a mechanical shutter interrupts the light beam until the film and the rotating mirror are positioned to start the exposure of the next row of dots, the advancing of the film taking place while the mirror is rotating into position to expose the next row.

Table 6-6 lists the four possible plotting modes. In each mode the diameter of the point of light on the film is equal to the resolution (5 or 10 mils). This produces a continuous image rather than an array of dots. The

Table 6-6. LGP 2000 Operating Modes

MODE	RESOLUTION, MILS	VARIABLE DENSITY	BITS REQUIRED PER SCAN
A	5	16 shades*	32,000
B	5	Black/white	8,000
C	10	16 shades*	16,000
D	10	Black/white	4,000

*Intensity mode.

plotting may be in black and white (black-and-white modes) or in 16 shades of gray, varying from black to white (intensity modes).

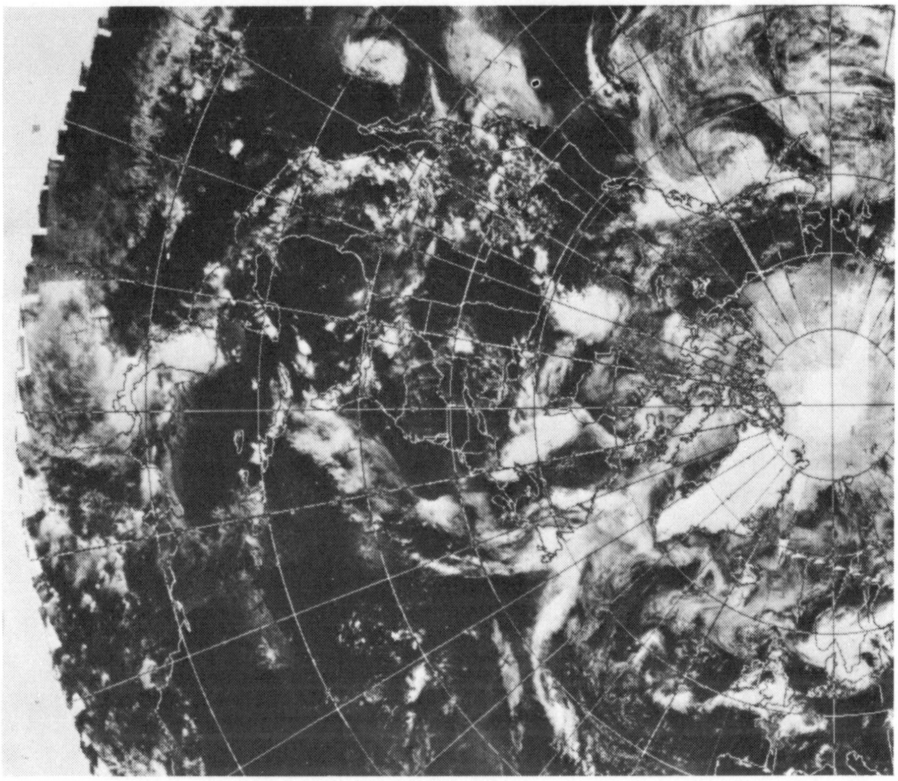

Fig. 6-7. Partial satellite weather map plotted by an LGP 2000 (July 8, 1968).

Applications

The LGP 2000 is generally suitable for applications in which the graphical display of digital data is required. The modes allowing display in different shades of gray can be used for halftone presentations, such as satellite weather maps. Dresser Systems states that the system is capable of metering out 100 feet of film continuously within the accepted tolerances for the geophysical plotting of 40-inch sections. Typical applications include—

1. Alphanumeric, high-speed displays.
2. Geophysical cross sections.
3. Continuous tone or line cartographic displays.
4. Contour maps.
5. Engineering drawings.
6. Graphic and tabular displays.

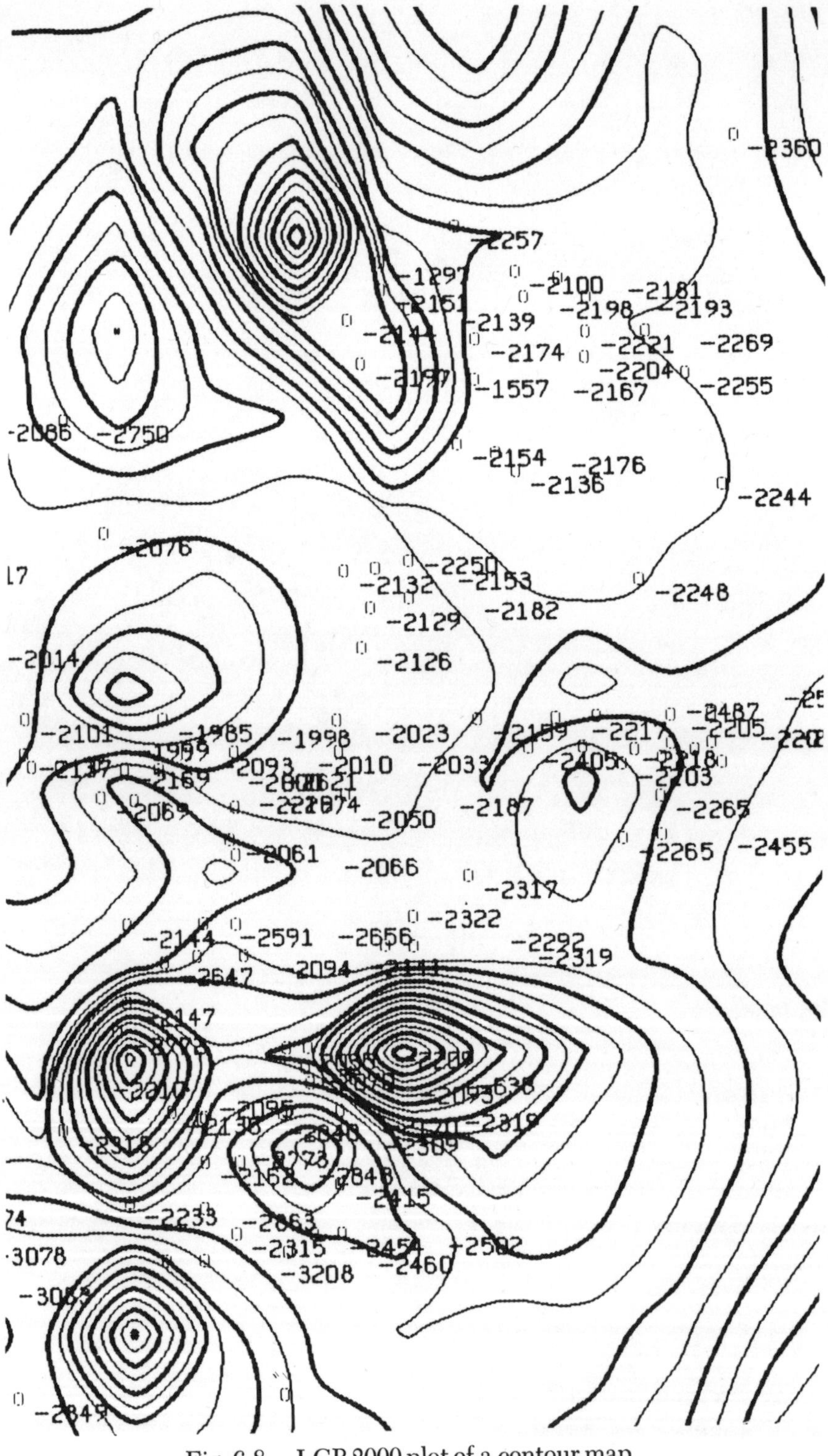

Fig. 6-8. LGP 2000 plot of a contour map.

7. Waveform analysis.
8. Aerospace and satellite flight dynamics displays.
9. Isobar-type weather maps.
10. Organizational and electronic schematic presentations.

Samples of LGP 2000 output are shown in Figures 6-7 through 6-9.

Input Requirements

The LGP 2000 always operates directly from a digital computer, even in the so-called off-line mode. The plotter accepts commands and binary data

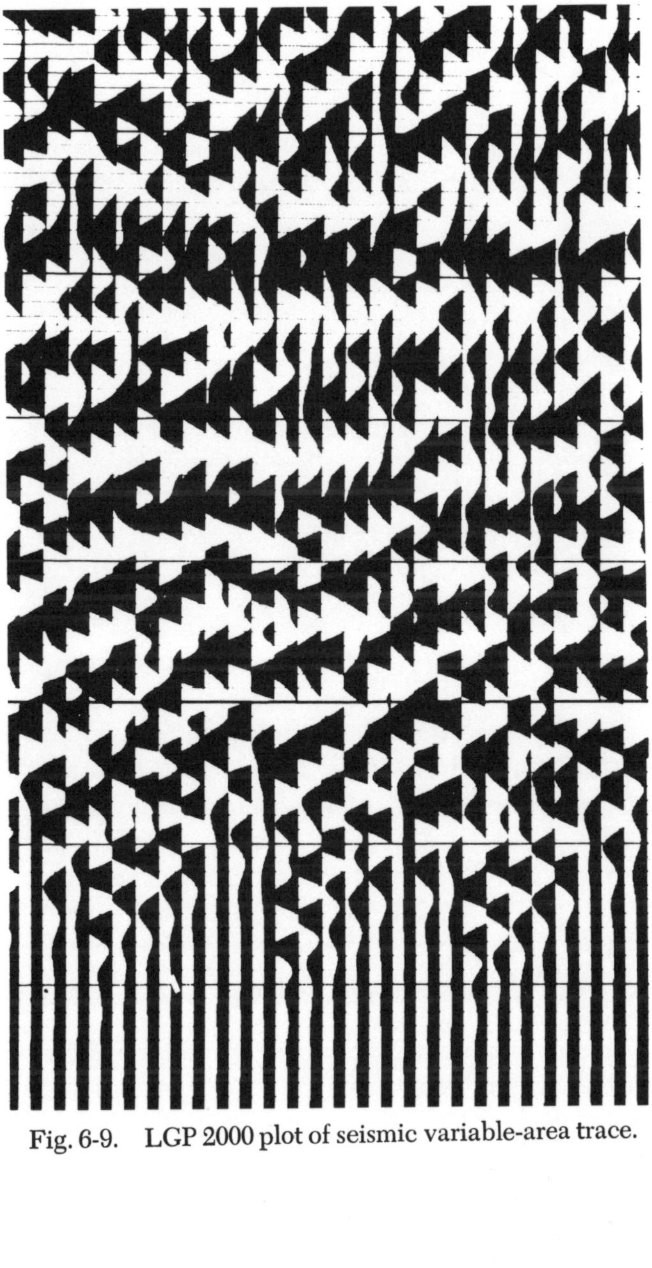

Fig. 6-9. LGP 2000 plot of seismic variable-area trace.

for plotting and returns status indications to the controlling computer. The *commands* recognized by the plotter and the status indications it returns are as follows:

1. Busy.
2. Channel end.
3. Device end.
4. Set 5-mil mode.
5. Set 10-mil mode.
6. Write black/white.
7. Write variable intensity.
8. Write specified intensity.

The *status indications* include–

1. Step film (advances film up to 256 steps as specified by a data byte).
2. Cut film (advances film 10.24 inches before cutting).
3. End plot.
4. Overrun (error condition).
5. Mirror stop (error condition).
6. Film stop (error condition).
7. Plot mode off (error condition).
8. Laser off (error condition).
9. Interlock open (error condition; cabinet not closed properly).
10. Film low.
11. Unit check (error condition).
12. Film service (error condition).

Program and Format

The LGP 2000 cannot operate directly with data generated by a user's computer program because the plot geometry information produced by the user program must be reformatted to suit the scanning action of the plotter. The reformatting process is described in the succeeding paragraphs.

The plot-generation process is shown schematically in the lower part of Figure 6-10. The final plot-generation process consists of reformatting an ordered input tape into the binary form required by the plotter. The plotter usually operates on line to the host computer (on-line mode) and is provided as a standard for IBM/360 computers, but systems for other computers are available. Details of the required IBM/360 configuration are given later.

An alternative way of operating is somewhat misleadingly called the off-line mode. Here the plot-generation software is used to produce a binary image of the plotting information on magnetic tape; the image is then

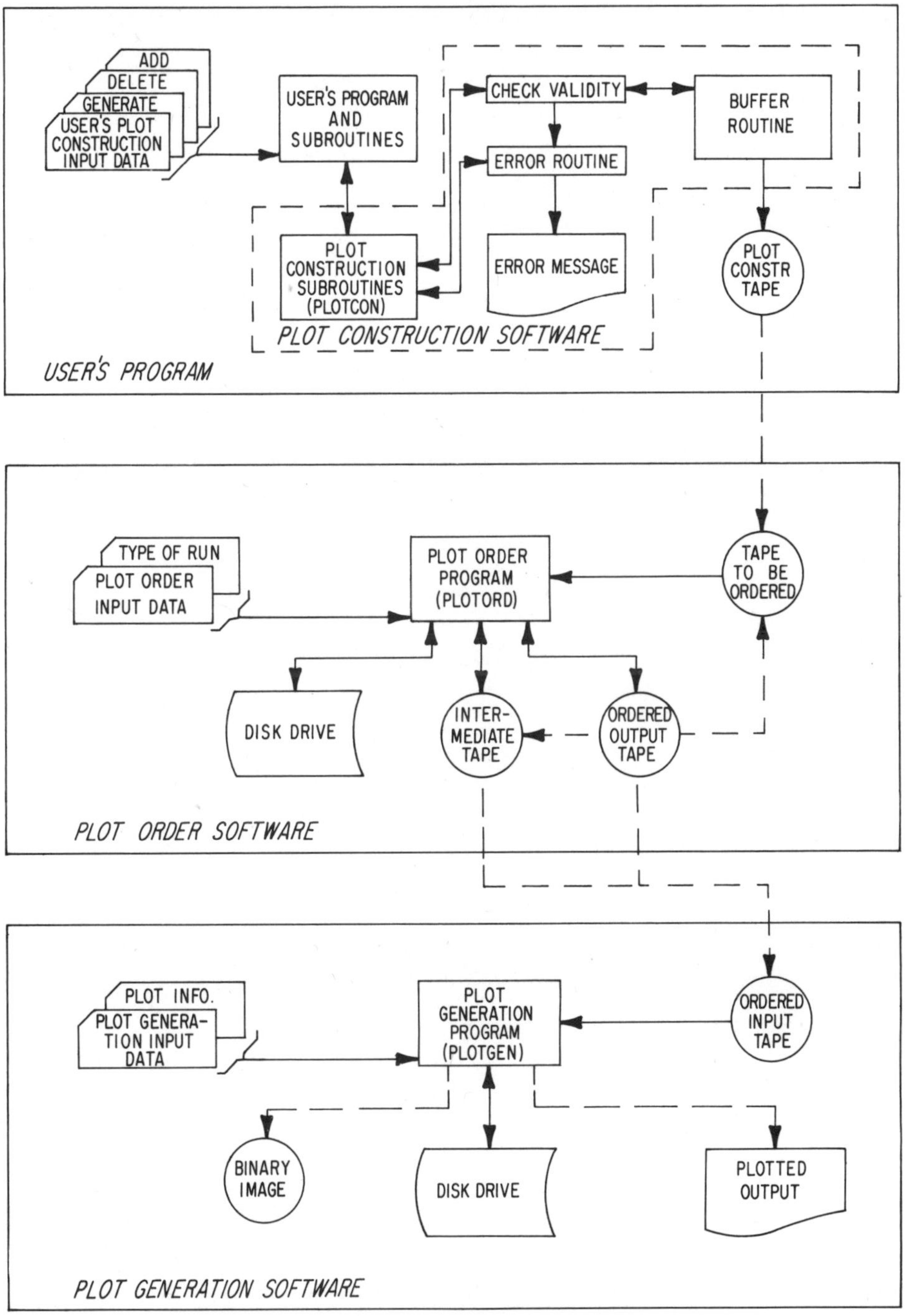

Fig. 6-10. Schematic diagram of LGP 2000 software.

plotted on another computer dedicated to operation of the LGP 2000. (See Table 6-5.) The function of the computer in off-line mode is simply one of transcription from magnetic tape to the plotter and coordination of the devices.

Software

Two different software series are provided for the LGP 2000 by Dresser, namely, general software and the seismic application package. The LGP 2000 *general software* consists of a series of subroutines and programs covering all stages needed from the initial user-program specification of the plot geometry to the final generation of the plotted output. The general software is arranged in three levels, which must be run sequentially to produce a plot. These stages are plot construction, plot ordering, and plot generation. Their operation is shown schematically in Figure 6-10.

The LGP 2000 *plot construction software* consists of a collection of FORTRAN subroutines to be called by the user's computer program. Available routines include—

1. Initial setup for establishing the position and scale relative to the plotter of the user's coordinate system (cartesian coordinates are used with axes parallel to the plotter axes); for establishing boundaries of the user's coordinate area within which all data must be displayed; and for selecting a user option that determines action to be taken if incorrect data is found during the plotting.
2. Subroutines for the output of continuous or dashed straight lines between specified points.
3. Subroutines for the output of symbols selected from a standard character set, strings of symbols, and straight lines consisting of repetitions of a specified symbol; the size, thickness, and orientation of each symbol can be designated.
4. Subroutines for the output of circles and circular arcs.
5. A subroutine for the generation of a solid polygon with specified vertexes.
6. Subroutines for the output, in characters, of fixed or floating-point numbers.
7. A subroutine to terminate the current plot.

The plot construction software produces output on a magnetic tape for subsequent processing by the plot-order software.

The LGP 2000 *plot order software* consists of a computer program that takes one or more tapes produced by the plot-construction software, including additional former plot-construction tapes for insertion or correction if required, and generates a plot-construction tape for use by the plot-generation software. Details of the tapes involved in the particular run are specified on a control card. Plot-order software uses two scratch tapes (i.e., work tapes) and a disk area for its internal processing. The IBM/360 minimum hardware complement for operation of the plot-order software consists of 65,536 bytes of core storage, one 2311 disk, two 9-track magnetic tape units, and one 7- or 9- track tape unit for the input tape.

The LGP 2000 *plot-generation software* is a computer program fed by the plot-construction tape, which is generated by the plot-order software. It creates either a plot on film if the LGP 2000 is operated on-line or a binary tape used as a signal source in off-line LGP 2000 operation. One control card specifies the input parameters for the run. These parameters specify the devices involved, the number of plots to be produced, the resolution of the plot and the intensities of the foreground and background of the plot. (The last of these specifications enables designation of negative plots at this point.)

The minimum IBM/360 hardware complement for the operation of the plot-generation software includes 65,536 bytes of core storage, one 9-track tape drive, one 2311 disk, and an on-line LGP 2000.

The LGP 2000 *seismic application package* is special-purpose software that processes trace-sequential seismic data on magnetic tape. The output tape is used later to drive the plotter for the production of standard geophysical representations. Specified by control cards, options in running the program include variable area, variable density, wiggle trace, variable area-wiggle trace, and variable density-wiggle trace. The seismic section plotted may occupy an entire roll of film. Options specifiable when the program is run include the use of timing lines, the scale and resolution of the plot, and the polarity of each of the traces. An annotation tape may be prepared using the general-purpose software and merged with the seismic trace produced by the seismic package.

Output from the seismic application package may be either sent directly to an on-line LGP 2000 or written on magnetic tape for off-line operation.

Output Characteristics

Output Modes

Plotter operation is the same for both the on-line and off-line modes. In both cases, binary data for the plot in process is transmitted to the plotter through the computer-plotter interface.

The four operating modes listed in Table 6-6 reflect the four combinations of black/white or shaded gray working and 5- or 10-mil resolution.

The number of data bits required for one complete pass from left to right across the film varies according to the operating mode and is shown in the right-hand column of Table 6-6; 1 data bit per point is required for the black/white modes of working, and 4 data bits per point are required for working in 16 shades of gray. See Table 6-7 for data rates and plotting speeds attainable with the LGP-2000.

Symbol Printing and Output Media

Although there are no special hardware capabilities for symbol printing, standard software for the LGP 2000 includes character output subroutines that can be used by a computer program generating plot information.

The output medium is Kodak Type 2496 film, which is roll film 42 inches wide and 100 feet long. This film is one of a series of Kodak films designed for rapid recording and high-temperature processing. The plastic film base gives good dimensional stability. Maximum size changes occurring in the film are given by:

1. Humidity coefficient of 0.003 percent per 1 percent relative humidity change.
2. Thermal expansion coefficient of 0.001 percent per 1°.
3. General limitation of ±0.03 percent size change during processing.

Three methods of film processing available from Kodak are as follows: conventional three-step processing; Kodak Monobath processing, which is a faster, more expensive method utilizing simultaneous developing and fixing; and machine processing. Machine processing for high-volume appli-

Table 6-7. Optimum LGP 2000 Operating Rates for Various Computer Data Channel Capacities

		MAXIMUM MIRROR SPEED, RPM; CORRESPONDING FILM ADVANCE SPEED, INCHES/MIN			
MODE:		A	B	C	D
RESOLUTION TYPE:		5-MIL INTENSITY	5-MIL BLACK/ WHITE	10-MIL INTENSITY	10-MIL BLACK/ WHITE
Computer	275,000	230;4.6	475;9.5	460;18.4	950;38.0
Channel	300,000	250;5.0	475;9.5	500;20.0	950;38.0
Peak data	800,000	475;9.5	475;9.5	950;38.0	950;38.0
Transfer Rate, bytes/sec	1,200,000	475;9.5	475;9.5	950;38.0	950;38.0

cations is provided by the Kodak Supermatic processor Model 242, which handles film 42 inches wide in rolls up to 18 feet long at rates from 2 to 12 feet per minute. A piece of film 42 x 60 inches is completely processed in about 90 seconds. Processing includes developing, fixing, washing, and drying.

Plotting Process

As shown in Figures 6-6 and 6-11, a laser beam is modulated and focused prior to falling on one face of a square mirror assembly. As the assembly rotates, it sweeps a spot of light deflected onto the film from left to right. As the laser beam passes across the film, it is pulsed to expose a row of dots. When a pass across the film is complete, a mechanical shutter interrupts the beam of light until the film and the mirror are in position to start the scanning of the next row, the film being advanced by a stepping motor. This sequence is repeated until the full length of the plot has been exposed.

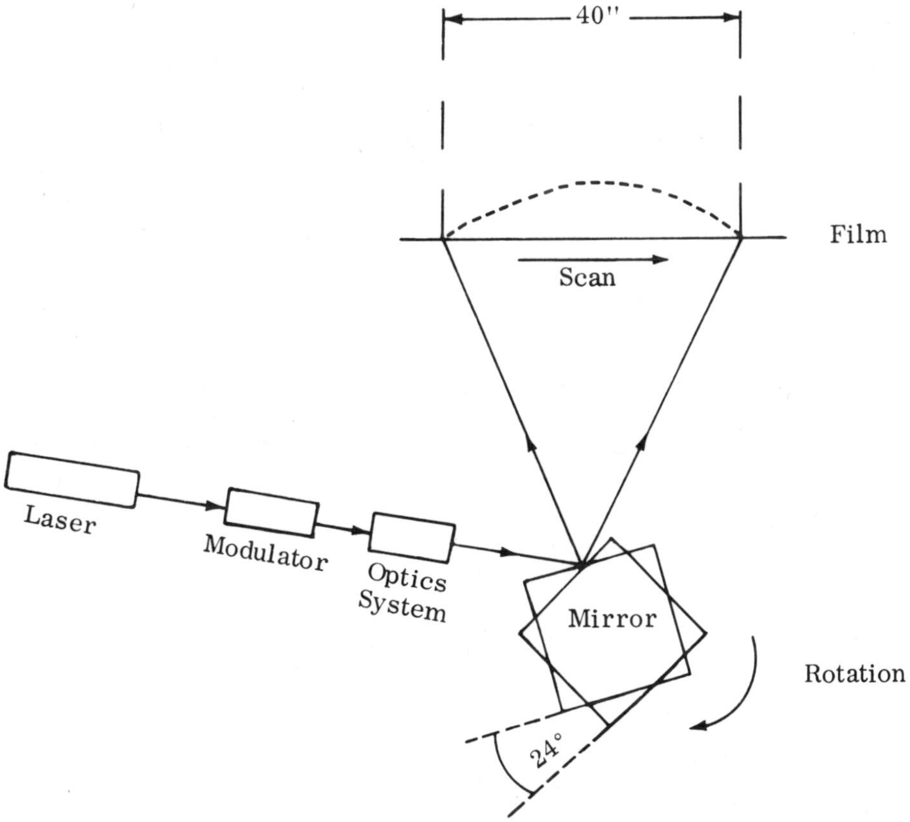

Fig. 6-11. LGP 2000 light-path geometry.

As shown in Figure 6-11, the rotating beam exposes a flat film; both the distance from the mirror to the spot and the speed of spot motion vary during a scan from left to right across the film. The variation in the distance from the mirror to the spot is negligible optically because of the depth of focus. The fluctuation in speed on this film, however, means that the laser pulsing speed must be coordinated with the angular position of the mirror to produce equally spaced dots on the film. The film stepping motor and the mechanical shutter must likewise be coordinated with the mirror position so that the beam is interrupted and the film advanced during the dead periods of the mirror rotation, when the mirror is not in the right position to deflect the spot of light onto the film. These coordinations are accomplished by control signals transmitted to the laser pulsing control, the mechanical shutter, and the film stepping motor from a magnetic drum attached to the shaft bearing the rotating mirror assembly.

Besides the mechanical shutter and the necessary lenses, the optics system includes a variable-density filter, which keeps the beam intensity at a preset level, and a modulator, which varies the intensity of the beam relative to its preset incidence strength in accordance with the input data. Other components of the optics system compensate for temperature changes.

The operating speed of the LGP 2000 is usually determined by the peak data-transfer rate of the computer data channel. The inherent speed of the plotter is governed by the mirror-assembly rotation rate and the action of the shutter, modulator, and film stepping mechanisms.

It follows that the mirror speed for operation of the LGP 2000 should be chosen to maximize the operating speed of the device, with regard to limitations imposed both by the characteristics of the LGP 2000 and by the peak data-transfer rate of the computer channel to which it is attached. Each LGP 2000 is provided with three different mirror speeds, selected either by the operator or by the program.

PART II—IMAGE DIGITIZERS

7. INTRODUCTION TO IMAGE DIGITIZERS

BACKGROUND AND DEVELOPMENT

The action of an image digitizer is opposite that of a digital plotter; that is, an image digitizer converts to digital form the shape of the path followed by some kind of sensor. This means that image digitizers make it possible to manipulate graphical information and supply it in the form of computer data. A wide range of applications of this capability exists, ranging from computer analysis of data recorded in strip-chart form to the use of elaborate systems that employ both image digitizers and digital plotters for the computer input, storage, modification, and output of precision maps and engineering drawings.

Early digitizers were developed for the reduction to digital form of analog telemetry data recorded on strip charts. Although this particular application has been largely superseded by the development of digital telemetry, low-cost digitizers of the same type are still available; these are digitizer analogs of strip recorders. The strip chart is driven at a constant rate beneath a cursor mounted on rails, while the operator moves the cursor up and down to follow the trace. The cursor position is read from a potentiometer, and the resulting voltage passes through an analog/digital converter to generate the digital output.

Such simple digitizers operate in one axis (i.e., dimension) only; the majority of present digitizers are two-axis models, although three-axis digitizing is also available. There is another difference in approach between the majority of current digitizers and the type just described; the position of the cursor is usually detected by direct digital means—such as through shaft encoders—to avoid inaccuracies due to voltage drift, which would limit analog digitizer resolution.

A typical modern digitizer, then, is a two-axis device with a cursor that is free to move over a flat working surface. The position of the cursor is detected digitally for output to cards, magnetic tape, a computer interface, or some other machine-readable digital form. A device of this type is shown in Figure 7-1.

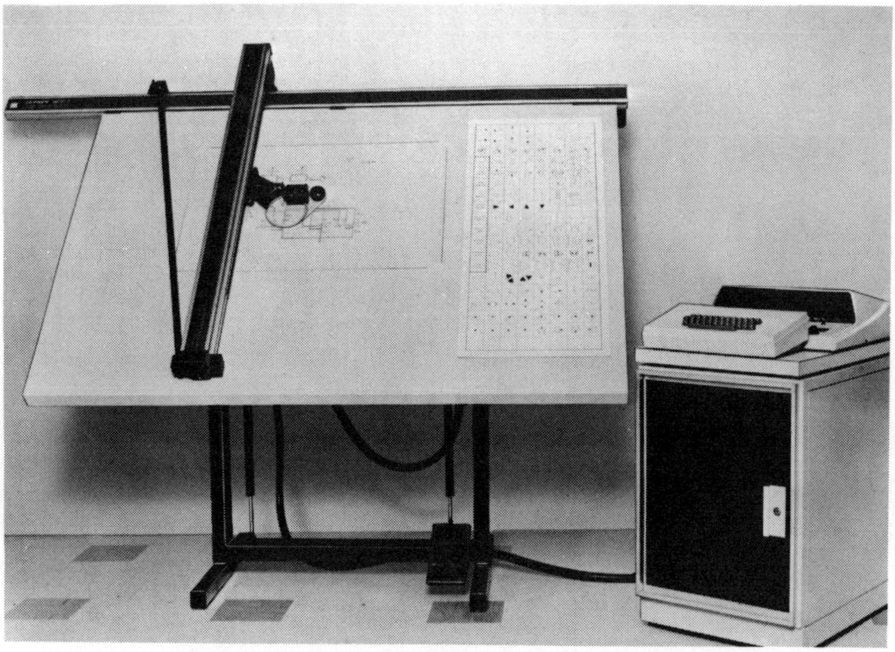

Fig. 7-1. Gerber GCD-1 coordinate digitizer.

Besides the two-axis digitizers, which account for most of the currently available devices, a number of units exploring unconventional digitizing technologies as well as one-axis and three-axis types are available. More specialized digitizers include input devices for the graphic displays used in computer-aided design applications and digitizing attachments that allow large flatbed digital plotting tables to function as digitizers (some of the attachments use automatic digitizing techniques).

APPLICATION AREAS

The areas in which image digitizers are useful cover many diverse fields, which have little in common save a need to convert graphical data to digital form for computer processing. Simple digitizing of strip-chart records has applications ranging from telemetry to the digitizing of traces generated in such diverse fields as speech analysis, seismic prospecting, or medicine. Precision two-axis digitizing is used in the operation of automatic drafting systems, which at their most complex level are totally computer-based systems for the computer handling of engineering drawings. A system of this kind might be used to generate perspective or isometric drawings of an engineering part specified by two elevation diagrams or alternatively to perform scaling. Other functions of fully automated drafting systems may include calculations involving input of part drawings as data or the generation of tapes for numerically controlled machine tools, given drawings of the parts as data.

A related area concerns the maintenance of a computer library of graphical data on magnetic tape, using an image digitizer for input and a digital plotter for output. Maps can be maintained in digital form and modified; such a system might be used, for example, to update nautical charts. Any modifications to existing charts would be specified to the computer and completely current charts would be drawn from the resulting data when needed. Similar applications are the maintenance of up-to-date maps of highways and land subdivision boundaries.

Another function of systems using an image digitizer for input is the production of accurate drawings from rough sketches, saving large amounts of drafting time. This has been applied specifically to the drawing of electronic-circuit diagrams and to the preparation of photographic artwork for printed-circuit boards and IC masks, using a digital plotter with photographic plotting capabilities. This is a particularly important market area for digitizers at the present time.

Three-axis digitizing has been applied to the computer input of data from stereoscopic photographs and to the digitizing of the shapes of design models used in shipbuilding, automotive, and aircraft industries.

Numerous applications require the digitization of photographic data, ranging from computer input of aerial photographs and x-ray photographs of tumors (for dosage calculations) to input for the computer processing of bubble-chamber photographs generated in high-energy physics experiments. As digitizers become more widely available, many new applications can be expected.

CLASSIFICATION

Because of the already extensive scope of digitizers on the market and the number of different device types in each functional area, it is difficult to generate a rigid classification scheme. However, the available digitizers may be roughly divided into small-scale flatbed and special-purpose units, with digitizing attachments for automatic drafting systems forming a separate category. Divisions outlined here are the basis for arrangement of the remaining chapters in this book: A thorough discussion of some currently available flatbed digitizers makes up Chapter 8, and Chapter 9 deals with the digitizing attachments available for automatic drafting systems.

Small-Scale Digitizers

These devices are used for small-scale manual digitizing and generally use the potentiometric method of digitization discussed in the first section of this chapter. Available devices vary from strip-chart digitizers, in which the chart is driven continuously below a fixed rail carrying the cursor, to simple two-axis digitizers that are placed on the drawing to be digitized.

An example of a simple two-axis digitizer is Bolt Beranek and Newman's Graftran, a small, potentiometric device in which digitizing is performed by moving a stylus over the selected drawing, the stylus being mounted on a telescoping arm that pivots through an angle of 110 degrees around the heavy base of the instrument. Both the angular position of the arm and its telescopic extension couple to potentiometers.

Another example of a small-scale digitizer is the Graph-Data DI-1400, in which the digitizing stylus connects to an arm joined to a two-wheeled carriage; digitizing signals are sent from the carriage to a paper-tape punch in the DI-1400 cabinet when a foot switch is depressed.

Flatbed Digitizers

The majority of available digitizers may be placed in a flatbed class, that is, units that have their own dedicated work surface. A typical digitizer of this type is the Gerber GCD-1, shown in Figure 7-1. The device consists of a controller connected to a work surface (called a coordinatograph), over which a handheld cursor moves freely. The arrangement of X-axis and Y-axis carriages (Fig. 7-1) in the device illustrates the arrangement of most of the flatbed digitizers available.

A disadvantage of the carriage arrangement is that the working surface is encumbered by the carriages; a number of manufacturers have devised techniques for avoiding this. The Bendix DATAGRID® digitizer* has a free cursor that interacts with electric signals in wires below the digitizing

*The name DATAGRID® is a registered trademark of the Bendix Corporation.

surface; the Gradicon graphic coordinate digitizer (GCD) has a carriage beneath the plotting surface which automatically keeps pace with the cursor.

Other designs aimed at increasing the accessibility of the working surface include the arm configuration of the Concord Control digitizer shown in Figure 7-2. A different arrangement again is used in the Boston Digital LTD/1, illustrated in Figure 7-3; here the cursor is attached to wires reeled out from two corners of the work surface, the lengths of the wires being used to compute the cursor position.

The description of these devices as two-axis flatbed digitizers gives a restricted impression of their versatility. Many of them include provisions for three-axis digitizing, although in that case the digitizing tool holder must be provided separately.

A common way to attain three-axis digitizing is to operate with a stylus held in a numerically controlled machine-tool table, which provides digital readout of the tool position. Greater versatility in two-axis digitizing, compared to that of a standard coordinatograph, is provided by translucent working surfaces (for the digitizing of photographs using backlighting).

A notable example of a digitizer with great flexibility is the Graf-Pen, manufactured by Sciences Accessories Corporation. This instrument digi-

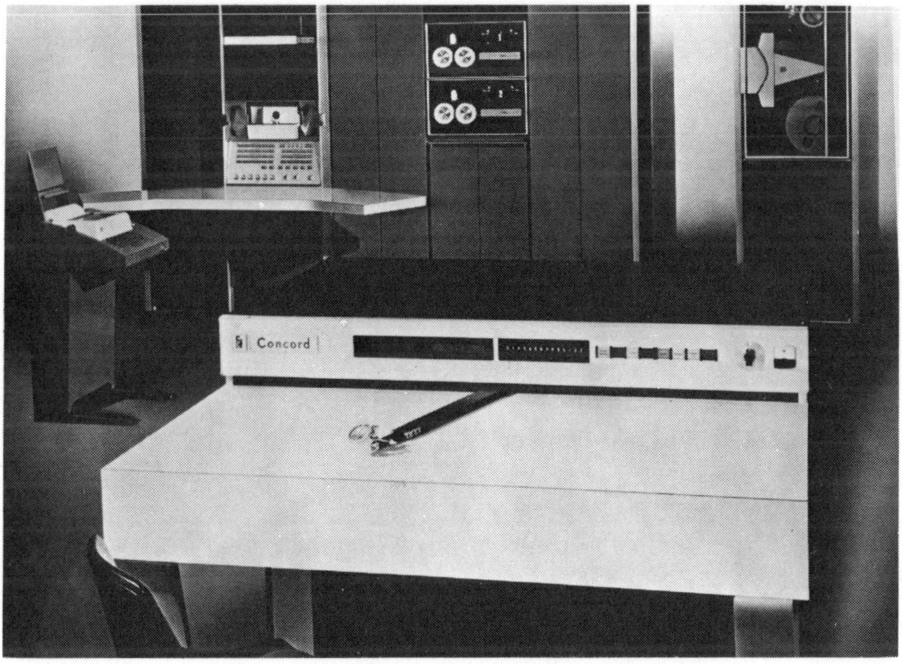

Fig. 7-2. Concord Control graphic data digitizer.

tizes by measuring the time of travel of an ultrasonic signal from the tip of the stylus to sensors placed along the edges of the working surface. Since this technique gives the work surface the passive role of supporting the sensors, any surface is acceptable; the manufacturer cites use of the pen to digitize an image on the face of a CRT and three-axis digitizing (using three sensors) of stereoscopic images viewed by the operator through special glasses. Graf-Pen has found its way into a number of novel applications because it is so broadly adaptable; it has even been used as a method of data input for questionnaire forms.

Digitizing Attachments

For large-scale flatbed digital plotters employed in a system where digitizing capabilities are also necessary, it is more economical to use a digitizing attachment for the plotter than to invest in a separate, freestanding digitizer. There are two different types of digitizing attachments for these systems, providing both manual and automatic digitizing capabilities.

Manual digitizing capabilities are provided by TV viewing heads. Closed-circuit TV allows the operator to watch the point below the digitizing head while operating controls to move the carriage. Automatic

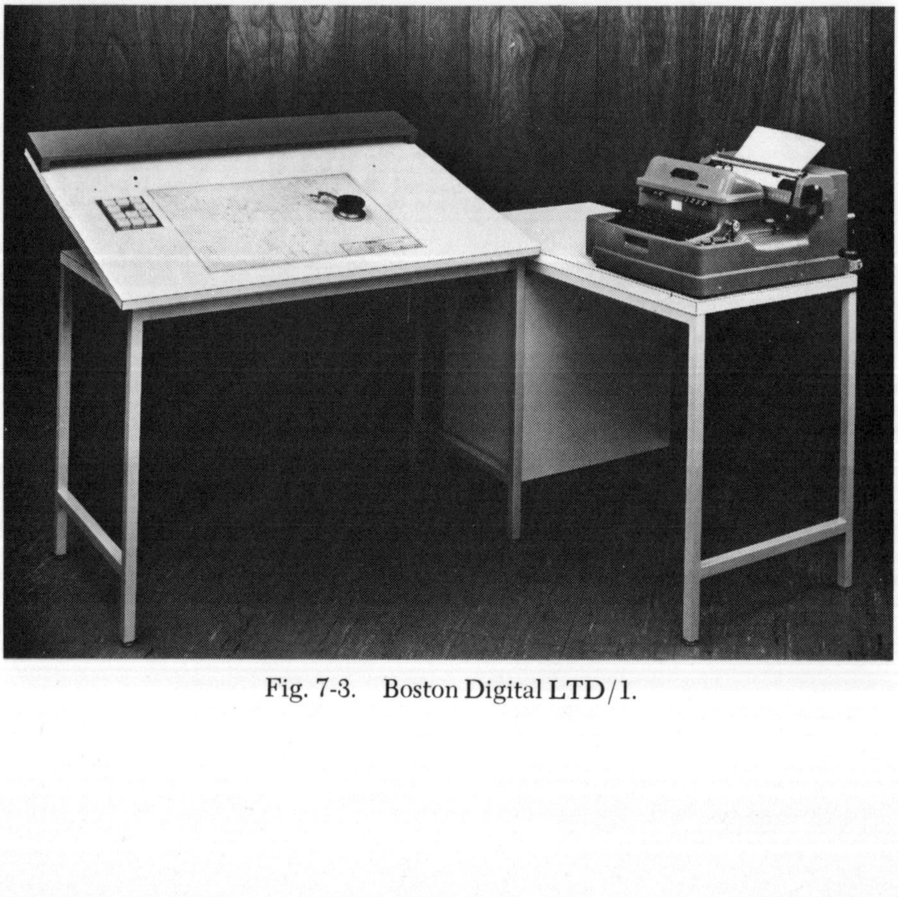

Fig. 7-3. Boston Digital LTD/1.

digitizing is possible through more sophisticated devices that follow lines and curves automatically, requiring operator intervention only occasionally. These automatic digitizers incorporate some kind of continuous scan of the area beneath the digitizing head; mechanical scans involving a rotating mirror have been used, but a TV scanning process is now more common.

Special-Purpose Digitizers

Several special-purpose devices available may be classified as digitizers, although their specialization precludes their full consideration in a general survey of digitizers. One example is a flying-spot digitizer developed specifically for the digitizing of bubble-chamber photographs generated in high-energy physics experiments; the processing of the data collected from a single experiment may involve the examination of thousands of photographs of patterns of small bubbles. The flying-spot digitizers operate on line or off line. Each photograph is subjected to a scan of the kind used in generating a television picture, and the coordinates of every bubble found during the scan are digitized for subsequent processing.

A variety of digitizing devices has been developed for the specific purpose of providing operator input of graphic data for graphic displays. These are interactive displays that generate graphics on a viewing screen

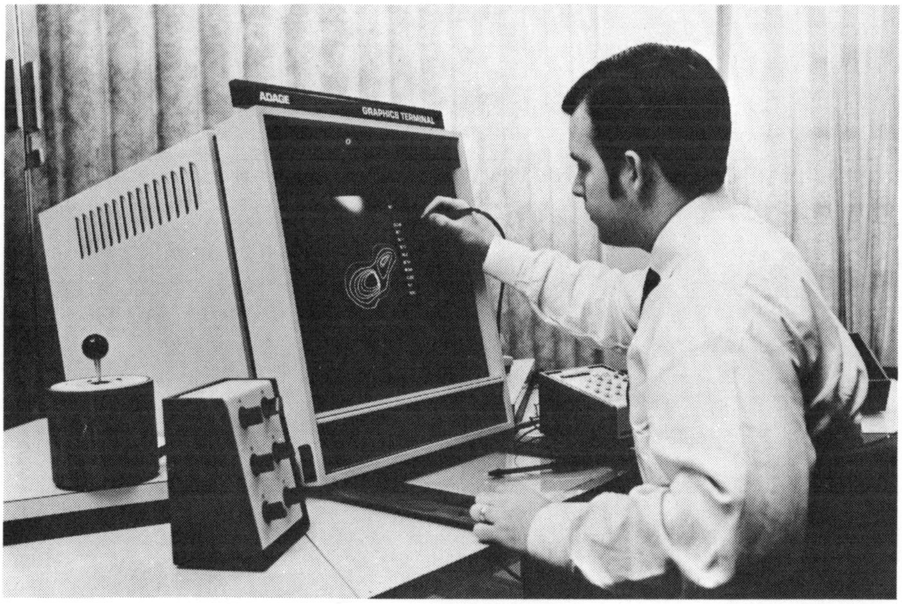

Fig. 7-4. An Adage graphics terminal, including joystick, variable control dials, light pen, Adage data tablet with stylus, and function switches.

for modification by either the computer or the operator. The prime application of these displays has been in computer-aided design, but other research areas include display of the results of computer simulations in real time (for example, a dynamic display of the view from an aircraft during landing), and the display of stereoscopic views of complex molecules responding to stresses.

Input devices for graphic displays are designed for maximum operating convenience. Their resolution, however, need not be great, since the screen of a graphic display is divided into raster cells; there are rarely more than 2048 raster cells in either direction, so the whole range of points to be digitized extends only over 11 bits in each coordinate.

Figure 7-4 shows an Adage graphics terminal with an assortment of operator input devices. The cursor on the screen may be moved manually by means of the joystick control to the left of the photograph, while the tablet in front of the operator digitizes the track of a metal stylus by using its tip to detect signals generated in a rectangular grid of wires beneath the writing surface. A light pen, held by the operator, communicates to the computer the position of the displayed point on the screen at which it is directed.

A light pen operates by sensing a flash of ultraviolet light when the

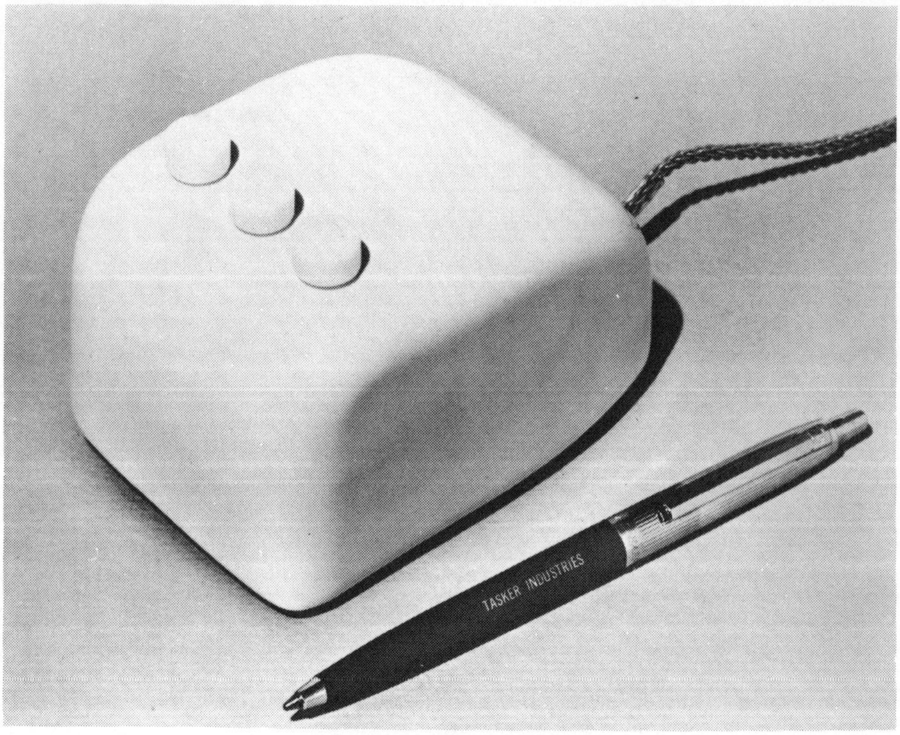

Fig. 7-5. Tasker mouse.

point in front of the pen is regenerated by the computer display-maintenance procedure. When this flash is detected, a signal is sent from the pen to the computer, which enables the computer to identify the point at which the pen is directed.

Another type of special-purpose digitizer is a wheeled "mouse" that fits under the operator's hand and generates digital signals as it is moved across a flat surface; a mouse by Tasker Industries is shown in Figure 7-5.

Since the preceding devices are peripheral to the use of graphic displays, they are more appropriately included in a full discussion of graphic displays than as a part of a discussion of digitizers. There is, however, a commercial digitizer based on a Rand tablet, the first tablet developed for use with graphic displays. This digitizer is the Bolt Beranek and Newman Grafacon, shown in Figure 7-6.

In the Grafacon there is a grid of wires below the working surface, each of which receives a different set of electric pulses at regular intervals. Pulses sensed by the stylus are used to detect its current position; as a check, the operator is informed if the stylus moves more than the distance between two adjacent wires during regular intervals of stylus detection.

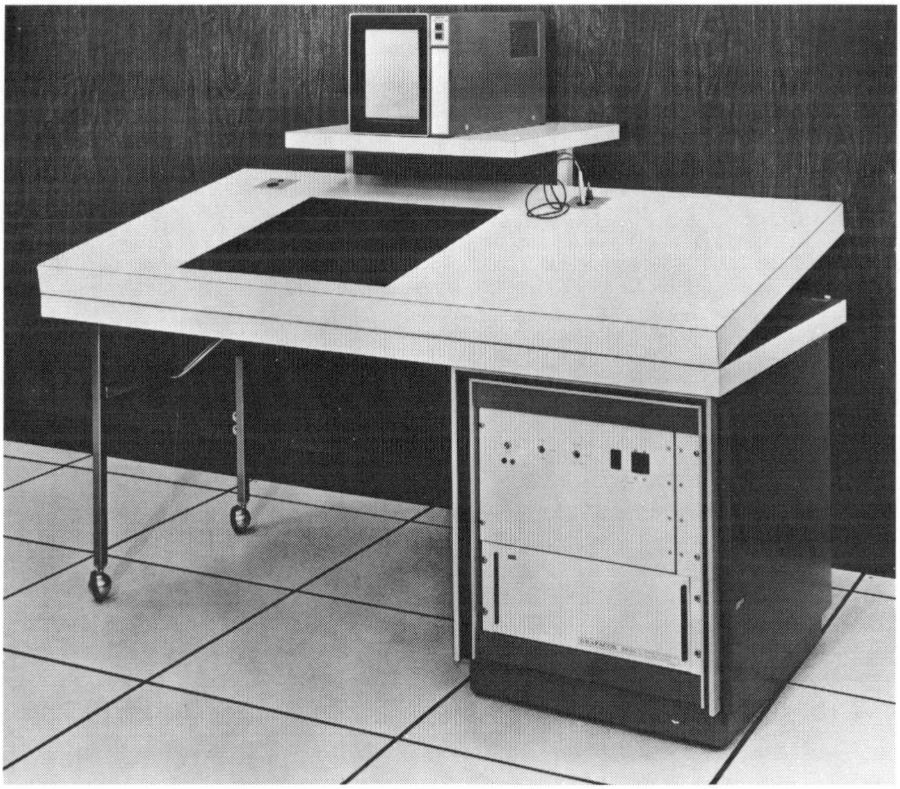

Fig. 7-6. Bolt Beranek and Newman Grafacon 2020.

OPERATING AND SYSTEM CONSIDERATIONS

Since an image digitizer is essentially a medium conversion device, digitizers are not used in isolation but in conjunction with other system components. When a digitizer unit is viewed as part of a complete system, some considerations arise with reference to digitizer operation and the output form; in a computer-based system, the digitizer mode of operation and output depend ultimately on the software used. Subsequent paragraphs are based on system considerations that arise in connection with two-axis manual digitizers, but similar points apply to the use of any digitizer.

The process of following a curve with a cursor is highly susceptible to random operator errors, which arise from the inevitable failure of the operator to follow the precise line being digitized. Where accuracy is essential, as in the digitizing of an engineering drawing or a map for computer manipulation and subsequent regeneration on a digital plotter, random errors can be minimized by digitizing the same data a number of times and using computer smoothing techniques to minimize random errors. This procedure naturally requires suitable software.

In the context of random operator errors, note that there are a number of digitizer applications in which accuracy is not particularly important. An example is the use of a computer to generate precise drafting or electronics artwork from rough sketches: The operator might perform a crude digitizing of a rough drawing of an electronic circuit diagram, which is then refined by computer processing and finally drawn accurately on a digital plotter. Similar techniques have been applied to the computer generation of finished photographic masters from rough sketches, the artwork being produced photographically on a flatbed digital plotter (discussed in Chapter 5).

Data for electronic circuit diagrams or artwork frequently contain large amounts of standard, repeated information, such as the symbols of an electronic component type or a connector pad in a printed circuit. (Other uses of standard symbols in drawings that can be digitized and regenerated by computer are found in engineering drafting and welding drawings.) In these cases it is clearly an inefficient technique to digitize each symbol as it occurs, so computer software has been developed to accept coded requests for standard symbols interspersed with the digitization of the drawing to be processed. Sometimes this is done by having the operator provide a keyboard code for each standard symbol he encounters.

Another approach, which is considerably simpler for the operator, is to place a diagram showing standard symbols over a part of the working surface away from the drawing being digitized. Each symbol is enclosed within a square, and the digitizer operator specifies a standard symbol by digitizing the point on his drawing where the symbol is to appear, followed by a point within the square containing the symbol on his standard diagram. The computer software examines the coordinates of each digitized point and interprets those falling within the symbol boxes as calls for the appropriate symbols. (The diagram does not necessarily need to be in a standard place on the work surface; the software might allow the operator to start operation by digitizing the positions of the corners of the diagram he is using.) This is a widespread digitizing technique, known as a "menu."

A "menu" is shown on part of the working surface of the Gerber GCD-1 digitizer in Figure 7-1; Gerber's DRAFT AID software package for the computer generation of precise drawings from sketches is discussed in Chapter 6 in the context of software for Gerber automatic drafting systems.

Output from a digitizer used in a computer-based system may be in one of several machine-readable forms, typical examples being punched cards, paper tape, magnetic tape; or it may be a direct connection to an on-line computer. For maximum system flexibility, most digitizers provide a range of customer options that affect the precise form and format of the output. Often, the exact output format is determined by the wiring of a replaceable patchboard, a board wired to customer specifications and which plugs into the digitizer and can easily be replaced to change the output format.

A more fundamental consideration in digitizer output is the type of information digitized. Most simple digitizers operate in a point mode, which means that the operator presses a button or a foot treadle whenever a point is to be digitized; the current coordinates of the cursor are then digitized.

Even within this single mode of operation, considerable variation is possible, depending on the way in which the digitizer functions in the particular system. Frequently, the manufacturer provides digitizer options that include switches for reversal (i.e., mirror image) of either axis, as well as scaling selection options that allow a choice of scale factors to be incorporated in the coordinate readings before output. The coordinate readings themselves may also be absolute (relative to a fixed origin) or relative (representing displacements from the previous point digitized) and can be automatically rounded to a preset grid resolution.

Although the point mode of digitizing is the simplest, it is tedious because operator action is required at each digitized point. It is also unsuitable for applications such as curve following, where the operator would have to estimate the number of points needed for adequate representation of the curve shape.

Other digitizing methods, available for some current digitizers, include modes for automatic digitization at present preset grid intervals or when the distance of the cursor from the previous digitized point reaches a preset value. A time-based automatic digitizing method has also been offered, wherein automatic digitizing of the cursor position takes place at fixed time intervals for as long as an operator foot control is depressed. It cannot be emphasized too strongly that the choice of digitizing method is not simply a function of operator convenience or of the type of information being digitized; it must be also related to the characteristics of the computer software used for processing the digitized data in the system as a whole.

8. FLATBED DIGITIZERS

INTRODUCTION

As already discussed, currently available digitizers encompass a wide range of device types, costs, and technologies, ranging from simple single-axis digitizers for the digitizing of strip charts to digitizing attachments for large precision-drafting systems or three-axis digitizers for use in conjunction with numerically controlled machine tools.

An important area of the digitizer market, and the one on which most manufacturers are concentrating, is the provision of two-axis digitizers with their own working surfaces. Typical devices in this category have work surfaces up to about 40 x 60 inches and resolutions of approximately 0.001 inch. Their scope of applications is extensive, including such functions as the digitizing of maps, electronic circuit artwork, and engineering drawings. However, accurate digitizing of large working drawings is usually accomplished by means of a digitizing attachment for an automatic drafting system, as described in Chapter 9.

Suppliers of flatbed digitizers include Auto-trol, Bendix, Boston Digital, Calma, Concord Control, Graph-Data, Gerber, and Instronics. In this chapter, three available devices are covered in detail as representative models: The thorough treatment of the Auto-trol 3800 illustrates the operation of the majority of the current devices, while the descriptions of Bendix and Instronics digitizers provide two examples of different approaches to digitizer design.

AUTO-TROL 3800 DIGITIZER

General Description

The Auto-trol Model 3800 digitizer, illustrated in Figure 8-1, converts coordinate data, usually from a 3939 Opti-Track® coordinatograph,* into digital form suitable for computer entry and subsequent manipulation. The operator moves the coordinatograph head across a drawing or some other graphical representation and pushes a RECORD button whenever the cursor is aligned with a point he wishes to digitize. Logic circuits convert the resulting electric impulses into computer-compatible, decimalized output.

An extensive patch panel can be wired in accordance with the desired output medium, which can be punched cards, paper tape, or magnetic tape. When the digitizer is to operate on line with a computer, output is delivered to a computer interface. If desired, an event counter can record the number of items digitized. Two models, 3800A and 3800B, are available. Model 3800A performs grid roundoff.

Figure 8-2 diagrams the signal flow of a typical system. As the operator moves the cursor, coordinatograph output pulses specify the amount of movement in the X- and Y-directions. When the RECORD button is pressed, a control pulse signals the console to output the coordinate data to the

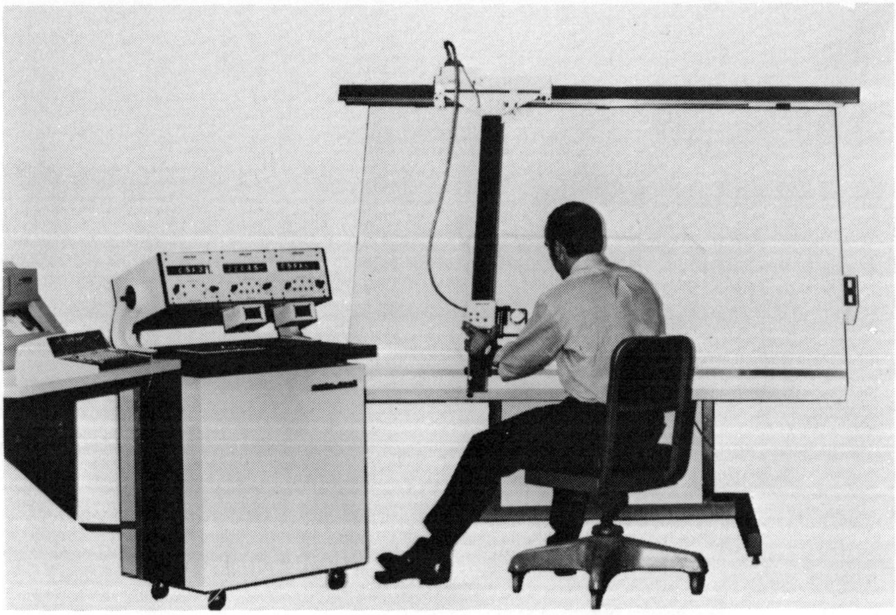

Fig. 8-1. Auto-trol Model 3800 digitizer.

*The name Opti-Track® is a registered trademark of Auto-trol Corporation.

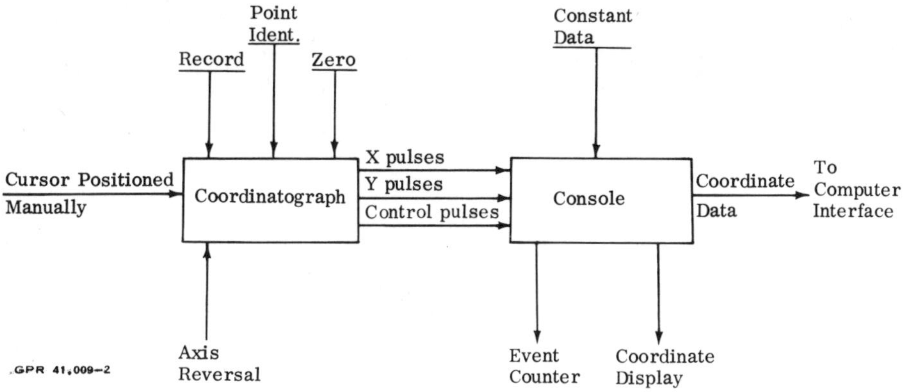

Fig. 8-2. System flow, Auto-trol Model 3800 digitizer.

computer interface or readout device. Pressing a ZERO button on the coordinatograph head sets the console counters to zero; the coordinate distances then measure from that point. X- and Y-axes interchange if the axis-reversal switch on the coordinatograph is pressed. Special points can be identified with the point-identification switch (optional).

In addition to transmitting coordinate data to the computer interface, the console exhibits it on nixie displays. Constant data can be inserted into the system by thumbwheels at the console. An event counter totals the number of record impulses. Some changes in system flow are possible to adapt the digitizer to special situations.

Applications

Like most digitizers, the Auto-trol Model 3800 is intended for applications that require rapid transfer of coordinate data from graphic form to computer input. Typical inputs are strip charts, engineering drawings, films, maps, and printed-circuit layouts—in other words, any situation involving areas or volumes to be compared or coordinate data from rough sketches to be refined and analyzed. The manufacturer claims particular market acceptance of the digitizer for printed-circuit and integrated-circuit applications.

Operating Controls

Coordinatograph

The coordinatograph is the component directly in front of the operator in Figure 8-1. It resembles a large drawing board with X- and Y-carriages; in fact, installation of a pen in the cursor converts it to a functional drafting table. In its more customary function as the input mechanism for the Auto-

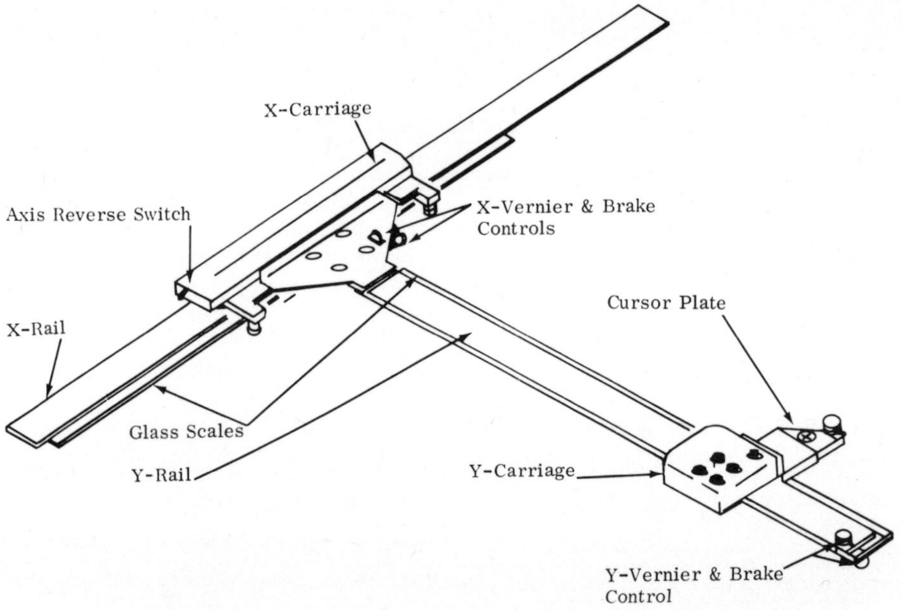

Fig. 8-3. Coordinatograph mechanism, Auto-trol Model 3800 digitizer (with Model 3939A X-Y Opti-Trak). (Reprinted with permission of the Auto-trol Corp.)

trol digitizer, the operator aligns the cursor with points on a drawing fastened to the table.

Figure 8-3 shows an isometric of the mechanism. The entire X-carriage rides on the X-rail as it moves in the Y-direction; the Y-rail, attached to and consequently moving with the X-carriage, supports the Y-carriage, which rides on it as it moves in the X-direction.

Figure 8-3 also shows glass scales attached to each rail. Not shown are two exciter lamps, one above each scale; two masks, one below each scale; and two photocells, one directly below each mask. Lamps, masks, and photocells move with the carriages; while in motion, the lines of the mask create a shutter action with the lines of the glass scale so that the photocell outputs two sine waves in quadrature. These are amplified, clipped, and sent as square waves to the digitizer counters, where they are counted and totaled as linear measurements of the head displacements.

One count may correspond to one, two, or four pairs of square waves, depending upon the setting of the scale switch. By responding to pairs of quadratured waves instead of single waves, the digitizer ascertains direction of carriage motion by detecting which square wave occurs first. Clearly, the counting mechanism can subtract as well as add, and therefore motion of the coordinatograph head need not be unidirectional.

In the Model 3939B coordinatograph, shaft encoders provide the measuring pulses. The graduated scales are disks rotated by rack-and-pinion drives as the carriages move along the rails. Photoelectric cells emit pulses, which are amplified and clipped as mentioned in the preceding paragraph.

The axis reverse switch (Fig. 8-3) interchanges X- and Y-pulses, X- and Y-verniers for fine setting of the cursor, and brake controls to lock one or both carriages. The latter are particularly valuable when motion must be restricted to one coordinate. Also seen in Figure 8-3 but not labeled are RECORD and ZERO buttons on the Y-carriage. As mentioned earlier, the operator presses these buttons to transfer coordinate data to the output recorder. Figures 8-4, 8-5, and 8-6 show the more common button arrangements. Each RECORD button calls for a different output format.

Console

Figure 8-7 shows how information provided by one pair of square-wave trains from the coordinatograph is handled by the console; data from the second pair of waves is handled by a second set of components. Only the data paths important to an overall understanding of system operation are described.

COUNTING. The two square waves from the coordinatograph enter the counter control at terminals 17 and 18. The counter control sends one pulse for each pair of waves to terminal 13 of the first up-down counter, which counts the pulses as they arrive until its nixie indicator reads 9, sends a pulse from terminal 14 to terminal 13 of the second up-down counter, and resets itself to 0 when the tenth pulse arrives.

It continues to count pulses until its nixie indicator again reads 9, sends a pulse to the second up-down counter (making it read 2), and resets itself to 0 when the twentieth pulse arrives. This goes on until the nixie for each of the two counters reads 9, corresponding to a count of 99 pulses.

Upon receipt of the next pulse by the first counter, a third counter receives a single pulse from the second counter; the first and second counters then reset to zero. Continued count involves a fourth and fifth up-down counter (not shown on the figure). Total capacity of the five-counter system is 99,999.

Terminal 12 of the counter control is wired to a corresponding terminal on each of the counters. When it is electrically negative, the counters will count in a positive direction; when it is electrically neutral, the counters will count in a negative direction. An indicator on the counter control exhibits the count direction. Terminal 15 of the counter control is similarly wired to a corresponding terminal on each counter; when it goes electrically negative, each counter resets to zero.

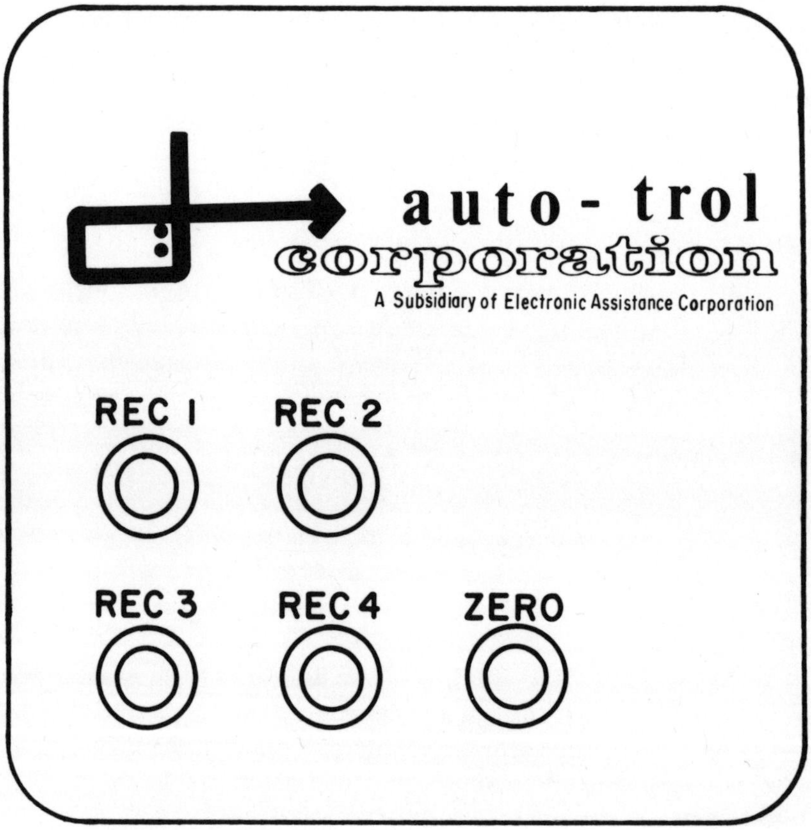

Fig. 8-4. Five-button "Y" carriage cover. (Reprinted with permission of Auto-trol Corp.)

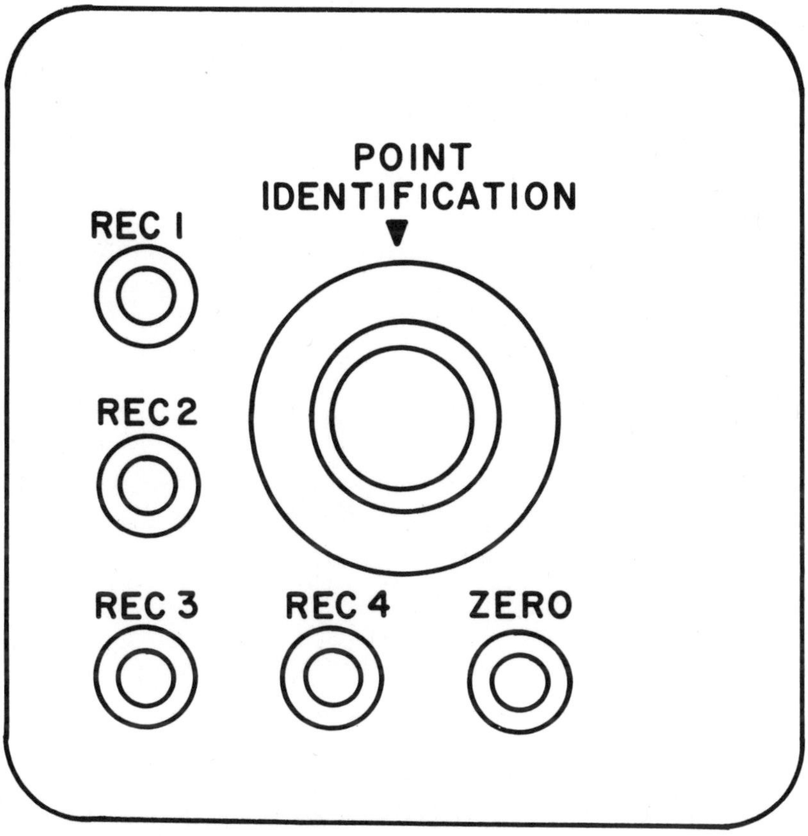

Fig. 8-5. Five-button with point-identification "Y" carriage cover. (Reprinted with permission of Auto-trol Corp.)

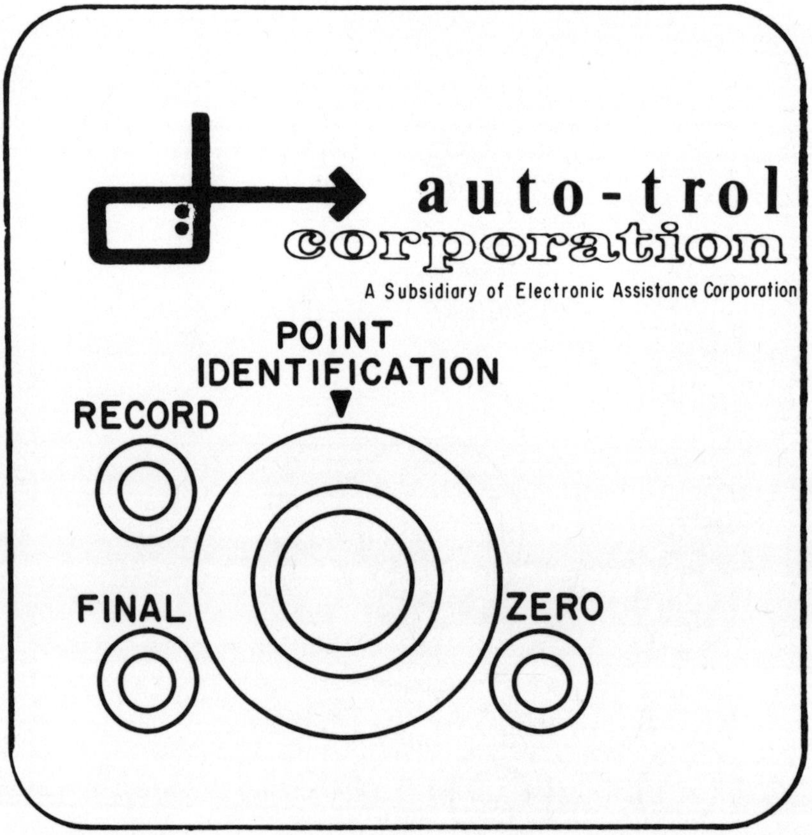

Fig. 8-6. Three-button with point-identification "Y" carriage cover. (Reprinted with permission of the Auto-trol Corp.)

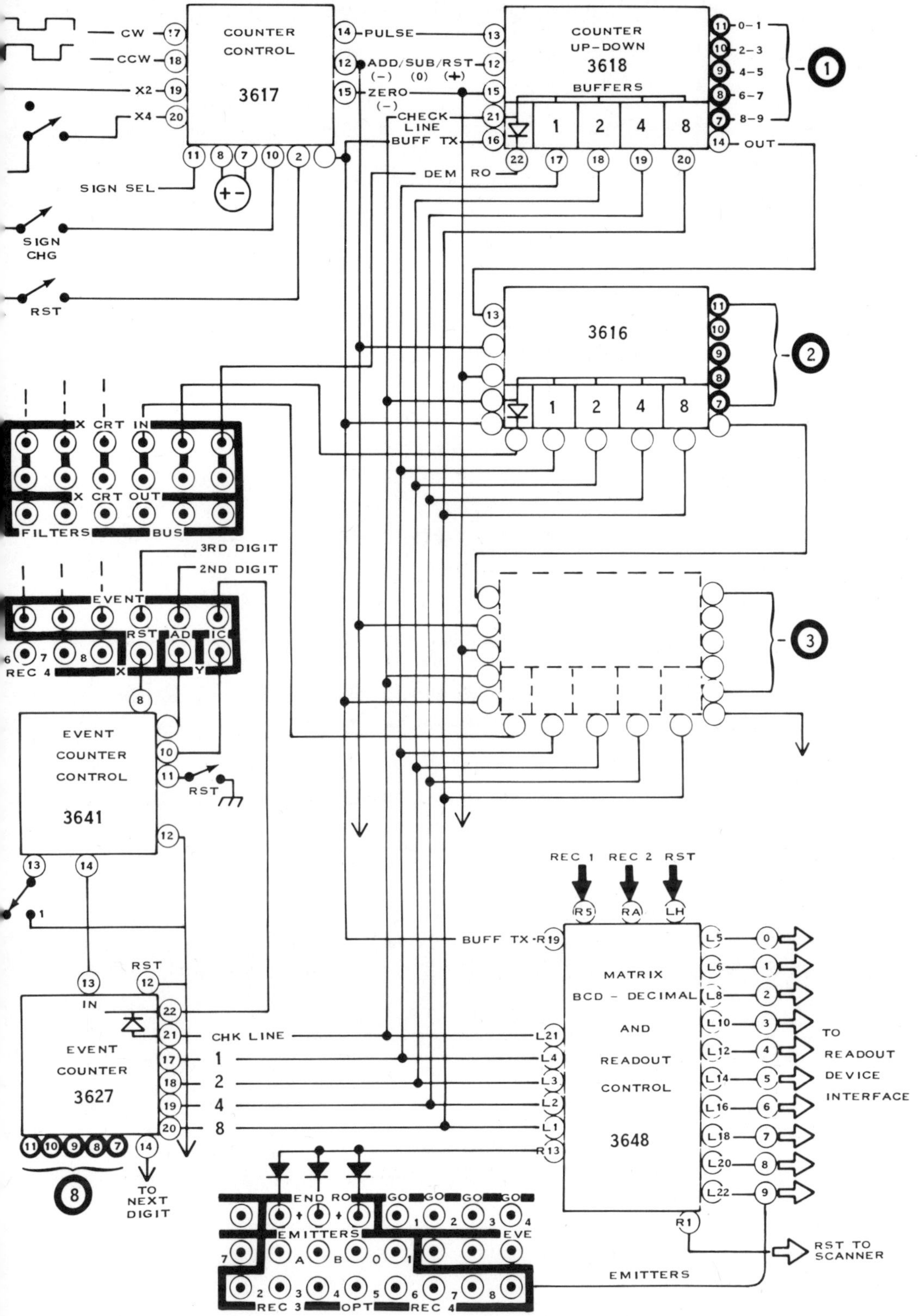

Fig. 8-7. Block diagram, Auto-trol Model 3800 digitizer. (Reprinted with permission of the Auto-trol Corp.)

Readout. The pulse count continues without effect on the console output until a record button on the coordinatograph is pressed. An electric signal is received at the readout control of the console, and an electrical connection between terminal R19 of the control and terminal 16 of the up-down counters transfers the reading of each counter into its buffer. From the buffers the readings are transferred to the readout control, where they are converted into decimal form in a bcd-decimal matrix and output to the readout device interface on ten lines, one for each digit.

An extremely important component of the digitizer—the patch panel—is also shown in part on Figure 8-7. The complete panel, shown in Figure 8-8, consists of a matrix of hubs that can be interconnected with plug-in (patch) cords to adapt the digitizer to different output formats. Because of the flexibility afforded by patching, each record button on the coordinatograph can initiate a specific output format when pressed.

The readings are retained in the buffers while being recorded by the readout device; as the operator moves the coordinatograph head, the counters continue to display new values without disturbing the buffers until a record button is pressed to transfer the new values into them.

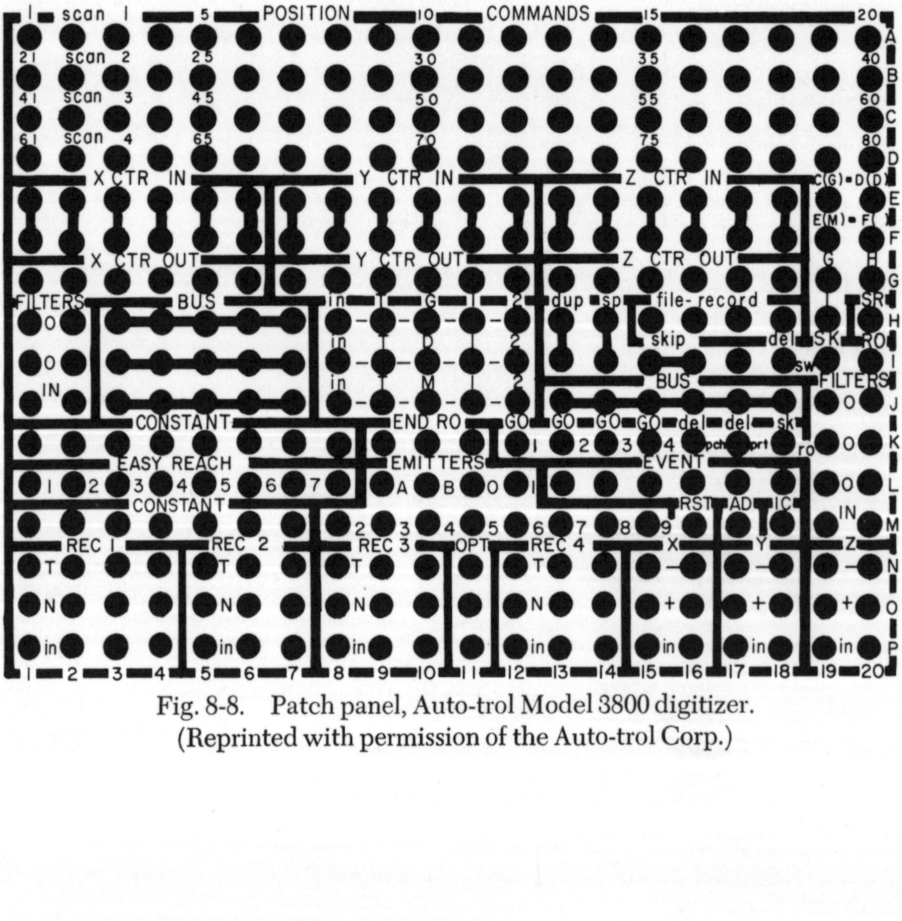

Fig. 8-8. Patch panel, Auto-trol Model 3800 digitizer.
(Reprinted with permission of the Auto-trol Corp.)

Normally, the buffers will not accept the new information until an end of readout signal is received by the readout control from the end RO bus of the patch panel (Figure 8-7). It follows that, although the operator of the coordinatograph can move the head to the next position immediately after pressing a RECORD button, the digitizer will not receive the new positional data until the data previously entered has been completely digitized and supplied to the readout devices.

EVENT COUNTER. A schematic representation of the event counter, its control, and the associated section of the patch board appears in Figure 8-7. This counter provides a record of events as directed by patch-panel programming; for example, it may be programmed to increment one for each data set. In a card punch system, the event counter often displays and records the card count.

CONSTANT DATA. Fifteen thumbwheel switches permit the insertion of a constant-data entry anywhere in the recorded format. Two sets of hubs, labeled CONSTANT in Figure 8-8, provide outlets from which constant-data elements may be patched to the desired output location.

Output and Options

Table 8-1 lists the various output devices compatible with the Auto-trol 3800 digitizer and their corresponding output media. Optional features include absolute and incremental coordinate recording (for preparation of direct input data for numerically controlled drafting machines and machine-tool directors), automatic readout (providing continuous recording at operator-selected increments without depression of the RECORD button), and various manual-entry keyboards.

Table 8-1. Output Choices for Auto-trol Digitizer Model 3800

OUTPUT DEVICE	MODEL	OUTPUT MEDIUM
Card Punch	IBM 024, 026, 029, 129, 526, Univac 1710	Punched cards
Pape-tape perforator	Auto-trol Model 5100	Paper tape
Flexowriter	Friden, Dura	Hard copy, paper tape
Magnetic-tape recorder	7- or 9-track, 1000 char./sec	7- or 9-track, magnetic tape
Direct interface to computers	IBM 1130, PDP-9, and others	On-line operation

BENDIX DATAGRID® DIGITIZER*

General Description

The Bendix DATAGRID® digitizer, shown in Figure 8-9, is an all-electronic, two-dimensional digitizer that converts the coordinates of graphic forms—such as maps, charts, diagrams, and drawings—into a digital code. This system is a departure from other digitizing systems in that it has no mechanical moving parts and thus eliminates the drawbacks of drag, limited movement, wear and tear, and frequent adjustment and calibration.

The work board, or surface, of the DATAGRID® is a white formica-covered grid of epoxy-encapsulated electrical conductors. Voltages are developed in these conductive strips by the action of an alternating magnetic field surrounding a coil situated in a cursor that is moved manually over a diagram on the work board. From these conductors the system logic circuitry receives input that specifies the coordinates of the cursor position, as defined by the particular conductor from which a voltage is accepted at a given instant. The system logic then processes the information to yield a digital real-time, two-axis readout of the cursor position. Finally, the digitized coordinates are transferred to paper tape, magnetic tape, cards, or a

Fig. 8-9. DATAGRID® digitizer with tape recorder.

Teletype. Hardware and software techniques can be introduced to compensate for misalignment, rotation, scaling, rounding-off errors, and biases in the coordinate-conversion function.

The active area of the work board is available in three different sizes: 30 x 36, 36 x 48, and 42 x 60 inches. The work surface is mounted on a drafting table that has both height and tilt controls. Digitizing resolution of the board is 0.001 inch, and absolute accuracy is ±0.005 inch. Repeatibility is ±0.001 inch.

Operating Controls

Input

CURSOR. The cursor, situated in an epoxy encasement, is a free-moving, handheld device that makes rapid tracing speed and high accuracy possible. It contains a coil that generates an alternating magnetic field from the electric energy supplied by an audiofrequency oscillator. This field cuts through the grid of conductors to induce voltages in them, the magnitude of which depends on conductor proximity. Four types of cursors are available as part of each system.

1. Reticle crosshairs inside a 1-inch diameter ring for general digitizing. Overall size is approximately a 2-inch circle.
2. Wide-view cursor for precision following.
3. Marking cursor with 2-inch view area for scribing and inking.
4. Pencil cursor for high-speed tracing and digitizing where maximum accuracy is not a requirement.

Four pushbuttons on the cursor control recording and coordinate initialization, and maintain the current coordinate.

KEYBOARDS. An operator can enter identification and machine language codes into the recording format via a 24-key keyboard. The keyboard is connected to the electronic circuitry by means of a ribbon cable that allows it to be moved anywhere on the work surface. Another keyboard containing 46 keys is available as an option. Thumbwheel switches are also available for entering constant, decimal, or numeric identification data into the output format.

OUTPUT. Interfaces are possible for almost any output device, depending on the user's needs. Data can be supplied to a Teletypewriter, card punch, seven-track magnetic tape, nine-track magnetic tape, or a paper tape punch. Output codes can be binary, ASCII, BCD, or EIA. Interfaces for conveying output to many different computers are also available.

PATCH PANEL. A removable 200-position patch panel is provided as a means of programming the sequence in which the characters generated by the system circuitry are to be recorded onto the output medium. Four formats are available, and a maximum of 40 characters can be recorded each time the appropriate mode RECORD button is pressed.

Modes of Operation

There are two methods of recording coordinate data: point mode and continuous mode.

Point-mode recording records the value of the X- and Y-positions with respect to origin each time a mode RECORD button is pressed. The coordinate values may be recorded as full values or as incremental changes from the previous recorded point, referred to as absolute or incremental mode recording, respectively.

In continuous mode, recording data can be recorded automatically in a continuous stream. Either of two such modes can be preset by the operator, namely, a time-base mode or a distance-base mode, both of which automatically trigger the recordings. The time-base continuous mode is variable from 1 second to the stepping speed of the recording device. In this mode, one recording is made for each time interval elapsed. The distance-base continuous mode is variable from X plus Y equals 0.001 inch to 0.999 inch. In this mode, one recording is made each time the specific distance is traversed.

Digitizing Process

The DATAGRID® digitizer was developed for high-speed digitizing through the elimination of problems inherent in an electromechanical system. Hence, this system is totally electronic and responds to voltages developed by the action of magnetic flux cutting a grid of conductive strips. The coil generating the field is mounted in a cursor, and it is energized by an audiofrequency oscillator. Thus, as the cursor is maneuvered over the work surface, voltages of various magnitudes are developed in the conductive strips.

Signals are applied to the electronic circuitry of the system each time a RECORD button is pressed or automatically at the conclusion of each preset time or distance interval. This information is then processed by the logic circuits and converted into a digital code. The coded output is recorded on paper tape, punched cards, or magnetic tape in the sequence programmed on the patch panel.

Operational Techniques

A number of techniques are available to the operator for manipulating the coordinates before they are transcribed onto an output device. He selects a common scale factor of either 1/10, 1/4, 1/2 or 1, and the system scales both axes to the value chosen. Independent scaling in each axis is effected by setting the proper scaling factors from 0.00001 to 1.99999 for each axis.

Another feature, known as grid recognition, achieves more rapid digitizing by automatically rounding off the point or path being digitized according to preset grid intervals. Coordinate rotation is carried out by rotating the electronic axes of the digitizer. The origin point of an X-Y coordinate system can be established at any point on the work surface.

Software

A library of basic software programs is available to do basic computational work. Capabilities include the determination of areas and volumes, lengths of straight or curved lines, angles, intersections, and clearances between mechanical components.

GRADICON GRAPHIC COORDINATE DIGITIZER

General Description

The Gradicon graphic coordinate digitizer, manufactured by Instronics Limited of Stittsville, Ontario, is shown in Figure 8-10. Like the Bendix DATAGRID® digitizer, the Gradicon unit is free of encumbrances on the

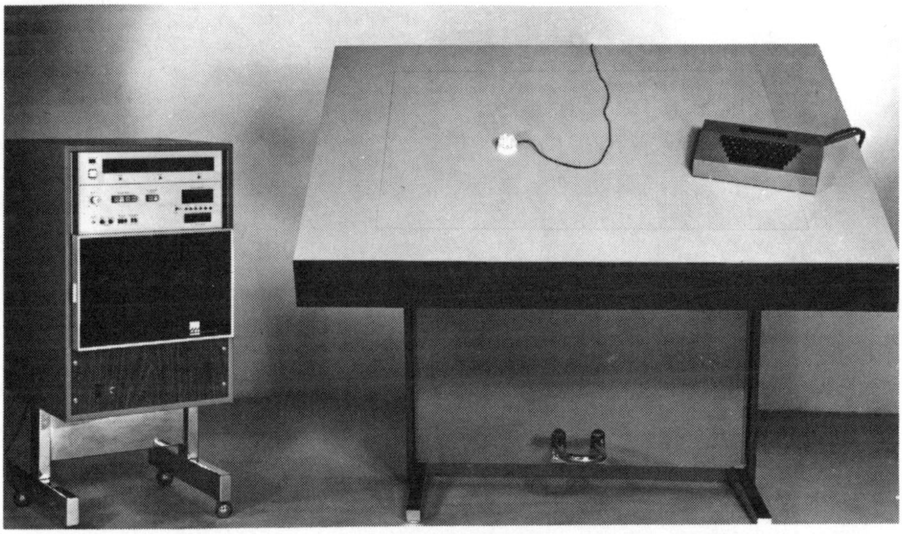

Fig. 8-10. Gradicon graphic coordinate digitizer.

digitizing surface. A graphical figure is placed on the digitizing table, and as the operator moves the cursor over its surface, an electromechanical, closed-loop servosystem drives a follower, located beneath the table surface, so that it reproduces cursor motion accurately. As the follower moves, it activates X- and Y-encoders, which send pulses to indicate follower motion to a controller. This unit processes them and outputs digitized coordinates indicative of cursor position. User-supplied output devices may include card punches, magnetic-tape stations, paper-tape punches, input-output typewriters, computers, and plotters.

Standard equipment includes digital coordinate displays with reset, four recording modes (time, point, incremental, and grid), absolute or delta coordinate values, scaling (1:1, 1:2, or 1:4), a 20-key keyboard for entering additional data, a handheld cursor with an operate switch, a foot-treadle operate switch, and a formatting patch panel with choice of six fixed characters.

EVALUATION. Design features emphasized by the manufacturer are obstruction-free table, high-response servosystem, convenient format change via patch board, easy convertibility to metric operation, and multiple interface capability. These make the Gradicon a very flexible machine.

In addition to making possible the obstruction-free table, the absence of mechanical coupling between cursor and encoders permits great freedom of cursor movement. Furthermore, the availability of different cursor types increases applicability range. The interchangeability of output devices is also an attractive feature, particularly if the optional removable patch panel is used.

Applications

In common with other digitizers, the purpose of the Gradicon is to convert graphical forms into digital data suitable for computer processing. The manufacturer stresses the following applications: computer-aided circuit design, seismological analysis, computer-aided tolerance studies, computer-aided stress studies, production of tapes for numerically controlled machine tools, computer-aided trend analysis, scaling of garment patterns, and analysis of meteorological records.

System Flow and Operating Controls

Figure 8-11 diagrams the data flow for the basic system. The pulse trains from the encoders (indicative of cursor position, as described previously) are used by the console circuitry to compute the X- and Y-coordinates of the instantaneous cursor position. These coordinates are continu-

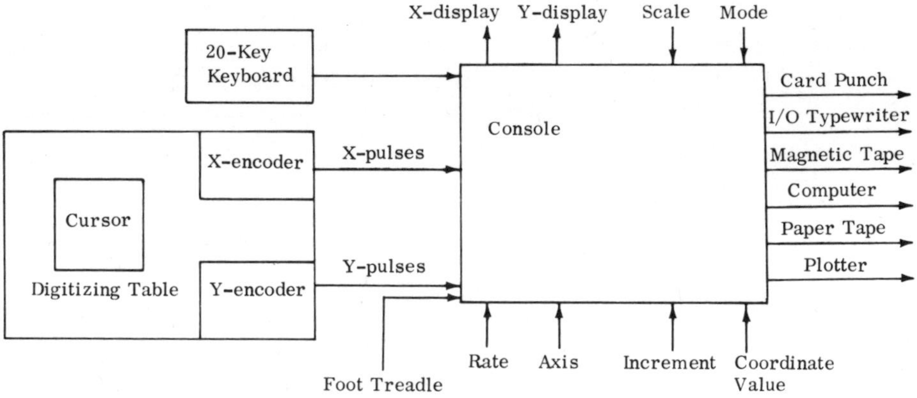

Fig. 8-11. System flow, Gradicon digitizer.

ously exhibited in the X- and Y-display counters, and are transferred to the output interface via a buffer and a patch panel.

The timing of the transfers depends upon which operating mode has been called for at the four mode pushbuttons. These are—

1. *Point mode.* X- and Y-coordinates are recorded each time the operator steps on the foot treadle or presses a RECORD pushbutton (not shown in Figure 8-11) on the cursor.
2. *Time mode.* X- and Y-coordinates are recorded at a preselected frequency as long as the foot treadle or CURSOR pushbutton is pressed.
3. *Grid mode.* The system approximates and outputs X- and Y-coordinates of cursor at closest intersection on a previously specified grid when foot treadle or CURSOR button is pressed.
4. *Incremental mode.* X- and Y-coordinates are recorded whenever cursor movement is equivalent to a preset increment.

The effects of certain controls on the input received at the Gradicon console are described as follows:

1. *Scale switch*: a three-position device that directs the Gradicon to digitize the X- and Y-cursor positions at full size, double size, or quadruple size.
2. *Rate switch*: a rotary device used in conjunction with the time mode to set the frequency at which cursor coordinates will be recorded.
3. *Axis buttons*: three pushbuttons used in conjunction with the increment mode to specify whether the increments at which the coordinates are recorded will apply for X- and Y-, or both X- and Y-motions of the cursor.
4. *Increment buttons*: two pushbuttons used in conjunction with the grid or incremental modes to specify the spacing (0.1 or 0.01 inch) between the imaginary grid lines.

5. *Coordinate value buttons*: two pushbuttons that set the system for absolute or delta operation. In the former, the visual readouts continuously display the distances of the cursor from a predetermined origin. In the latter, they display the distances from the previously digitized and recorded point.

6. *The 20-key keyboard*: permits the operator to identify coordinate values or to introduce extra data, usually for use in computer programming.

Digitizing Table

The digitizing table supports the graphical form on its obstruction-free surface. Below the table is an electrical coil that generates an electromagnetic signal sensed by a cursor held above the surface. The coil is mounted on a mechanical gantry; as the operator moves the cursor to follow the lines on the graphical item, two servomotors cause the generating coil to follow the cursor motion in the X- and Y-directions.

Cursor

As can be seen in Figure 8-10, the cursor is small and can be lifted away from the table and moved in any direction without constraint. It incorporates a coil that senses the signal generated by the coil under the table surface. As the cursor is moved, the generating coil repositions itself immediately under it, as described in the preceding paragraph.

Various cursors are available. An optional optical cursor (Gratilite) projects a graticule through the graphic material from beneath it. Other cursors are available for use with opaque material, images from overhead projectors, three-dimensional sources, and so on.

Console

The mobile electronics console houses the system control panel, display readouts, and the timing, synchronizing, and interfacing circuitry. Servoamplifiers and all power supplies are also housed there. Space is provided to accommodate a magnetic-tape transport.

Patch Panel

Itself part of the console, the patch panel permits an operator to interface the digitized output with any of the output devices. It comprises a set of plug terminals that can be interconnected by patch cords; bayonet spikes on the ends of the cords plug into receptacles in the terminals. Some of the terminals receive different items of digitized data; others carry signals to the output terminals; patch connections ensure that the items of data will be properly sequenced at the output terminals for the readout device being employed. Patching instructions are furnished by the manufacturer.

Output Devices

Any of the following output devices can be used with the Gradicon:

1. Card punch, IBM 029.
2. Card punch, Univac VIP 1710-04.
3. Magnetic-tape stations, 200, 556, and 800 bit-per-inch.
4. Paper-tape punch, 100 character per second.
5. Electric input/output typewriter.
6. X-Y plotter.
7. Various computers.

Optional Equipment

In addition to the special cursors described earlier, the following optional equipment is available for the Gradicon:

1. A removable patch panel permits rapid change of output configuration.
2. Z-axis coordinate readout display permits three-dimensional digitization.
3. Metric configuration permits use of the metric system.
4. Increased incremental selection permits changes in the digitization interval from 0.002 to 0.999 inch when operating in the grid or incremental modes.
5. A 43-key keyboard permits input of the full alphanumeric character set in place of the 20 characters obtainable from the standard keyboard.
6. Keyboard verifier provides a 16-character display of keyboarded information.
7. Fixed address thumbwheel switches permit addition of fixed data to the output.
8. A utility counter specifies number of digitizations that will elapse between each automatic incorporation of utility-counter data into the output.

9. DIGITIZERS AND AUTOMATIC DRAFTING

INTRODUCTION

It is easy to see that the large, sophisticated, computer-based, automatic drafting systems that produce engineering working drawings are greatly enhanced by the inclusion of digitizing facilities, for then graphic input to the system can be used for subsequent computer processing. Combined digitizing/plotting system capabilities are being used for computer generation of control tapes for numerically controlled machine tools and plotting of corrected versions of existing drawings.

Drawings that are digitized and stored within the computer can also be used as input to computer operations (for instance, weight and volume calculations); or they can be processed in some way for production of other working drawings, examples being the computer preparation of perspective or isometric views from design drawings showing elevations, and the computer scaling of drawings.

For small-scale work involving drawings up to about 40x60 inches, it is common to join the operation of a flatbed plotter with that of a flatbed digitizer of the type discussed in Chapter 8. When drawings are larger, however, the cost of providing separate working surfaces become excessive, and the usual approach is to provide attachments for drafting tables that enable them to be used as digitizers. It follows that in considering the applications of digitizers to automatic drafting systems, two different types of devices are of interest: the flatbed digitizers covered in Chapter 8 and the digitizing attachments provided for large flatbed digital-plotting tables.

Two variations of digitizing attachments are commonly provided for large digital-plotting tables: manual and automatic. Manual digitizing capabilities are provided by a closed-circuit TV system in which an operator manipulates controls to move the plotting head, guided by a TV monitor connected to a TV camera on the head. Crosswires centered in the viewing field indicate the precise point to be digitized.

TV camera heads for use in manual digitizing are available for automatic drafting systems supplied by Gerber, Kongsberg, Tridea, and Universal Drafting Machine. One version of the technique, which features a series of concentric circles engraved on a glass plate below the TV camera, has been used to generate control tapes for numerically controlled machine tools; the operator positions the head so that the circle whose diameter corresponds to that of the cutting tool runs tangent to the edge of the part to be machined. This method has been largely superseded by the development of computer programs for the production of tool-control tapes from digitized engineering drawings.

A more sophisticated digitizing capability is provided by automatic digitizers that follow a line automatically and output digitized coordinates; however, operator intervention is necessary at junctions or other points of difficulty. Because these devices are expensive and complex, they are important only to very large facilities where there is a high volume of digitizing work, but their mode of operation is of considerable technical interest. CalComp has produced an automatic digitizing attachment for its flatbed plotting systems that automatically follows the boundary between a light and a dark area, and standard automatic line-follower attachments are available for drafting systems from Gerber and Tridea. A comprehensive discussion of the Gerber automatic line follower concludes this chapter.

GERBER OLF-1 AUTOMATIC DIGITIZING SYSTEM

General Description

The Gerber Model OLF-1 automatic digitizing system comprises an optical line follower, a console, and a software package; it furnishes automatic digitizing capability to the Gerber 2032 or 2075 graphic display systems, two of the Gerber automatic drafting systems discussed extensively in Chapter 5. When operating in its digitizing mode, a head with an optical line follower automatically tracks the lines of a drawing mounted on the drafting table of the display system and sends coordinate information to the computer whenever programmed considerations are met.

In its drawing mode, a pen in the head traces the pattern corresponding

Fig. 9-1. Gerber OLF-1 automatic digitizer head.

to the digitized information, permitting easy verification of digitized data. Although originally intended for automatic operation, the system can be controlled manually as a point digitizer. A TV monitoring display is included.

The optical line follower is shown in Figure 9-1. Note the four fiber optics bundles below the head; these illuminate the area below the sensor and TV camera while keeping the hot light sources away from the working surface.

Figure 9-2 diagrams the data flow through the OLF-1 digitizer and the associated Series 2000 control. Cross-hatched blocks (line follower and console) represent the digitizer proper; plain blocks, the graphical display. To digitize a graphical item, the operator affixes it to the drafting table, slews the line follower manually until the TV display shows it aligned with the first digitizing point, and sets the follower in automatic operation. The follower then traces the lines of the item and outputs the instantaneous X-Y position every time it meets the conditions of the digitizing parameters. The control, programmed with Gerber's automatic digitizer program, outputs the digitized coordinate data to paper or magnetic tape.

In addition to slewing the line follower to its start position for automatic operation, the manual steering handwheels and the foot-operated speed control can choose between alternate paths. If the follower has

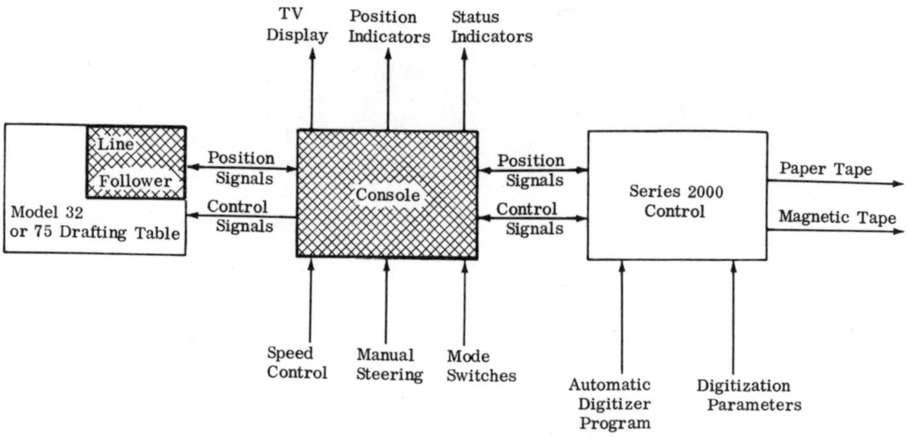

Fig. 9-2. System flow, Gerber OLF-1 digitizer with Series 2000 graphical display.

started to follow the wrong path from a junction, it can be backspaced to an earlier position. Most system controls are located at the console.

Manually controlled and semiautomatic digitization are also possible with the system. In the former, the operator uses the TV monitor (Figure 9-3) to follow the motion of the cursor across the drawing as he controls that motion by manual and foot-operated speed controls. In the latter, each time the output button is depressed, the follower moves to a point as far ahead of the digitized point as the previous point is behind it. In effect, the machine continues in the direction prescribed by its previous motion; the operator then adjusts the follower position until the TV monitor shows the crosshair positioned over the line being digitized, at which time he presses the OUTPUT button to digitize the new point.

EVALUATION. In common with other digitizers, the OLF-1 system provides rapid transfer of coordinate data from graphic form to computer input. Its completely automatic operation increases accuracy as well as throughput speed, making it particularly adaptable to such high-precision applications as preparation of tapes for numerical control of machine tools. In addition, the manufacturer claims particular applicability to computer-aided circuit design, tolerance studies, human engineering, and medical diagnosis.

Operating Controls

The OLF-1 system is flexible, since it can function under manual, semiautomatic, and fully automatic control. Cost considerations, however, will probably dictate the purchase of the less expensive, standard, manual digi-

Fig. 9-3. TV monitor for Gerber OLF-1 digitizing system.

tizers for installations that do not make extensive use of the automatic line-following technique.

Drafting Table

As part of the graphical display system, the drafting table consists of a flat surface to hold the graphical item being digitized and movable members to support the digitizing head so that it can follow the lines of the graphical item across the surface. Two tables are suitable: the Model 32 (high precision) and the Model 75 (high speed). On both tables the active drawing area is a rubber platen. Detailed descriptions of these drafting tables are included with the treatment of the full range of Gerber automatic drafting systems in Chapter 5.

Line Follower

The line follower of the OLF-1 digitizer is a vector generator that images a line from the graphical item onto a vidicon tube. The electron beam in the tube scans the tube face in the same manner that the face in a TV camera is scanned in broadcast television. As it sweeps across the face, its intersections with the line image are sensed and used to determine the slope of the line with respect to the point momentarily aligned with the follower axis. The follower then moves in the direction specified by the slope, the scanning continues to determine the line slope with respect to the instantaneous position of the follower, the direction of follower motion changes to reflect the new slope conditions, and so on. In this manner the axis of the follower traces the line. Photoelectric encoders transmit pulses representative of X- and Y-motion to the console, where the instantaneous X- and Y-coordinates of the follower are continuously displayed.

Although the photoelectric encoders transmit coordinate data continuously as the line is traced, output of the digitized line position occurs at discrete intervals specified by the Series 2000 control. This control, incorporating a minicomputer programmed with Gerber's automatic digitizer program, calls for data output whenever the criteria previously entered as digitization parameters are satisfied.

When functioning as a plotter, the follower moves across the table surface as commanded by input digitized data. It contains a station that can accommodate inking or scribing devices to produce the desired plot.

A crosshair reticle defines the exact coordinate position read by the photoelectric encoders, and a C-shaped slave reticle indicates the vector direction of the follower. Both reticles are visible on the TV display of the console. A zoom system permits continuous magnification variation to accommodate line widths that range from 0.008 to 0.975 inch.

Three operating modes are permitted. In the automatic mode, the system automatically follows the line as described previously. In the manual mode, the motion of the follower is controlled by a manual steering device and a foot-pedal speed control. In the mixed mode, the system operates manually until the head is positioned within 0.005 inch of a line. Then it locks onto the line and begins to follow automatically.

Console

The console comprises a television monitor, a foot-operated speed control, and a control panel. The TV monitor displays the C-shaped slave reticle and the crosshair reticle superimposed on an enlarged view of the working surface. Scanning rate is 729 lines per second; resolution is 500 TV lines per inch.

The foot pedal, which varies the follower speed from zero to maximum, is spring-loaded to return to a preset constant speed.

The control panel provides for the following inputs:

1. *Digitize on*: an on/off switch that activates the operator's control panel.

2. *Output on*: an on/off switch that signals the computer program to apply digitize criteria to the follower movement.

3. *Backspace*: a switch used by the operator to reposition the head over the point where the program last calculated a valid datum point. This switch is used when the output buffer is full or when the follower no longer sees a line. Pressing the BACKSPACE button returns the head to the last valid datum point, where line following continues without discontinuity or loss of data.

4. *Edge follow*: a switch that selects either the edge-following mode or the line-following mode.

5. *White/black*: a switch that selects between following white lines (or edges) on a black background and black lines on a white background.

6. *Stop at intersections*: an on/off switch to signal the program to stop the follower head at intersections.

7. *Proceed after intersection stop*: a pushbutton used after the system stops at an intersection.

8. *Readout*: a switch to force data output.

9. *X-position—Y-position*: positioning handwheels connected to pulse generators for fine positioning of the follower head.

10. *Manual steering*: a 360-degree manual steering device for normal slew control to guide the head through poor-quality areas, dash lines, or congested areas.

11. *Manual-mixed-automatic*: a three-position switch that selects the mode of operation.

12. *Quarter/full speed*: a switch interconnected with the speed control to permit finer control of the follower speed by providing quarter-speed at the fully depressed foot-pedal value.

Many of the switches also function as indicators, since they are backlighted to illuminate when the switch is in the "on" position. Indicator lights not part of a switch are—

1. *Lock on*: a light that illuminates when the follower head is locked onto a line.

2. *Buffer limit*: a light that illuminates when the output buffer is three-quarters full, signaling the operator to reduce speed to prevent overflow.

3. *Position indicators*: two coordinate display counters, each containing six electronic digital-display tubes (arithmetic sign plus five digits) that give the instantaneous coordinates of the head as it moves.

4. *Sequence counter*: a three-digit, unidirectional sequence counter that advances one each time the readout cycle is initiated.

GERBER SERIES 2000 CONTROL

Gerber's Series 2000 control is a stored-program, general-purpose computer with an 8K memory and a high-speed arithmetic option. It incorporates an operator's desk with a 10-character-per-second Teletypewriter (tape reader and punch), a 400-character-per-second photoelectric paper-tape reader, and a 10½-inch reel handler. A detailed description of the Series 2000 control is included with the treatment of the full range of Gerber automatic drafting systems in Chapter 5. For the OLF-1 system, an automatic digitizing program adapts the control for following lines or edges and outputting data in accordance with preset criteria, as required in an automatic digitizing system.

Software

The automatic digitizing program, supplied by the manufacturer, implements the digitizing hardware. Its features are described next. The entire program, including all features, must be stored in the memory of the Series 2000 control before the OLF-1 system can function.

Digitize Criteria

One very important function of the program is to specify the criteria by which the output intervals will be determined and to call for data output when the specified criteria are met. Four sets of digitize criteria are initially set into the program; selection of a particular set is made through the Teletypewriter on the control. A fifth set with undefined test limits is provided so that values not provided by the initial four tests can be specified at the Teletypewriter.

Table 9-1 presents a typical set of digitize criteria. The operator would

Table 9-1. Typical Digitizing Criteria

SET NO.	LENGTH, INCHES	SLOPE, DEGREES	AREA, SQ. IN.	CENTRAL ANGLE, DEGREES
1	1	20	No test	No test
2	1	20	0.00025	10
3	1	10	0.00006	5
4	1	10	No test	No test
5	Variable	Variable	Variable	Variable

call for set 1 when digitizing a graphic composed of straight-line segments; digitizing data would be output automatically any time the reading head moved more than 1 inch in the direction specified at the previous digitizing point or any time its direction of motion differed by more than 20 degrees from its direction at the previous digitizing point. Set 2 is for complex curves; in addition to output of digitizing data according to the criteria of set 1, the system will output it when the area between a straight line from the last digitizing point to the present cursor position and the actual line traced by the cursor becomes 0.00025 square inch, or when the circular central-angle deviation is more than 10 degrees. (The area deviation test is particularly suited to gradual curves, the central angle test to sharp curves.) Set 3 would be used for complex curves to yield closer datum points than set 2, and set 4 for straight-line segments to yield closer data points than set 1.

The importance of these digitizing criteria is evident, considering the amount of data that would appear without them. The sweep rate of the television vidicon tube in the reading head is 10,000 scans per second; therefore, if data were output every time the electron beam crossed a straight line, there would be 10,000 digitized points per lineal inch of travel at a typical speed of 1 inch per second. Since this is obviously too many, the preceding criteria that automatically adjust point frequency to drawing shape are used.

Other Control Parameters

In addition to the digitize criteria, the program provides for initialization and modification of other parameters from the input/output Teletypewriter keyboard or the low- and high-speed punched-tape readers. Selection from the following setup and operating parameters is provided:

1. *Scaling*: decimal scaling of coordinate data after correction for offset, separate for each axis, from 0.00001 to 999.99999 times.
2. *Offset*: decimal zero offset, separate for each axis, from zero to plus or minus 999.999 inches.
3. *Mirror image*: mirror image (sign reversal) calculation separate for each axis.
4. *Format detail*: output of absolute position or incremental distance coordinate commands with selection to a maximum word size of 3.5.
5. *Axis select*: selection of coordinate command addresses of two linear axes to be output from the drafting table.
6. *Sequence number*: automatic output of sequence number.
7. *Coding*: choice of output of EIA or ASC II codes.

8. *Parameter display*: display of current parameter values via type-out on Teletypewriter.
9. *Cutter offset*: automatic cutter offset from 0 to 99.999 inches.
10. *Parameter repetitive*: automatic output of additional word information in each block.

Output

Six-level paper tape is produced by the punch that is an integral part of the Series 2000 control. An IBM-compatible magnetic-tape unit can also be purchased to produce seven- or nine-level magnetic tape.

APPENDIX I: DIRECTORY OF MANUFACTURERS

Adage, Inc., 1079 Commonwealth Ave., Boston, Mass. 02215

Arvin Systems, Inc., 1771 Springfield St., Dayton, Ohio 45403

Auto-trol Corp., 6621 West 56th Street, Arvada, Col. 80002

Bendix Corp., Advanced Products Division, Bendix Center, Southfield, Mich. 48075

Bolt Beranek and Newman, Data Equipment Division, 1762 McGaw Avenue, Santa Ana, Calif. 92705

Boston Digital Corp., Main Street, Ashland, Mass. 01721

California Computer Products, Inc., 305 North Muller St., Anaheim, Calif. 92803

Calma Company, 707 Kifer Road, Sunnyvale, Calif. 94086

Computervision Corp., Northwest Industrial Park, South Ave., Burlington, Mass. 01803

Concord Control, Inc., 1282 Soldiers Field Rd., Boston, Mass. 02135

DATA TECHnology, Inc., 65 Grove St., Watertown, Mass. 02172

Dresser Systems, Inc., P.O. Box 2928, Houston, Texas 77001

Edwin Industries Corp., 11933 Tech Rd., Silver Spring, Md. 20904

Electronic Associates, Inc., 185 Monmouth Parkway, West Long Branch, N.J. 07764

Faul-Coradi, Inc., 27 Fennell St., Skaneateles, N.Y. 13152

Geo Space Corp., 5803 Glenmont Drive, Houston, Texas 77036

The Gerber Scientific Instrument Company, 83 Gerber Rd., South Windsor, Conn. 06087

Graph-Data Digitizing, 13834 South Prairie Ave., Hawthorne, Calif. 90250

Graphic Data, Inc., 169 Bedford St., Burlington, Mass. 01803

Graphic Systems Division, 14761 Califa St., Van Nuys, Calif. 91401

Hewlett-Packard, 1501 Page Mill Rd., Palo Alto, Calif. 94303

Houston Instrument (Division of Bausch & Lomb), 4950 Terminal Ave., Bellaire, Texas 77401

I/O Systems, 32 North Main St., Natick, Mass. 01760

Instronics Ltd., P.O. Box 100, Stittsville, Ontario, Canada

Kongsberg Systems, Inc., 10 DeAngelo Drive, Bedford, Mass. 01730

Mergenthaler Linotype Company, Mergenthaler Drive, Plainview, N.Y. 11803

Milgo Electronics Corp., Computer Graphics Division, 7620 N.W. 36th Ave., Miami, Fla. 33147

Omega-T Systems, Inc., 300 Terrace Village, Richardson, Texas 75080

Perspective Systems, Inc., 4400 Seventh Ave. South, Seattle, Wash. 98108

Science Accessories Corp., 65 Station St., Southport, Conn. 06490

Spatial Data Systems, Inc., 132 Aero Camino, Goleta, Calif. 93017

Time Share Peripherals Corp., Miry Brook Rd., Danbury, Conn. 06810

Tridea Electronics, 11581 Federal Drive, El Monte, Calif. 91731

Unitech Corp., 5 Daniel Rd., Fairfield, N.J. 07006

Universal Drafting Machine Corp., 5200 Richmond Rd., Bedford Heights, Ohio 44146

Varian Data Machines, 2722 Michelson Drive, Irvine, Calif. 92664

Xynetics, Inc., 6710 Variel Ave., Canoga Park, Calif. 91303

Zeta Research, 1043 Stuart St., Lafayette, Calif. 94549

APPENDIX II: COMPARISON CHARTS: DIGITAL PLOTTERS

The charts on the following pages present summary characteristics of currently available digital plotters. The Report Number entry in the charts indexes complete device coverage in *AUERBACH Graphic Processing Reports.*

IDENTITY		Arvin Systems 1197F2	Auto-trol 6030	Auto-trol 6035 Duo-trol	Auto-trol 6040
REPORT NUMBER		—	—	60.009.02	60.009.03
TYPE		—	Flatbed	Combination flatbed and drum	Drum
DRIVE SYSTEM		Servo chain	Stepper motors	Stepper motors	Stepper motors
USABLE PLOTTING AREA INCHES		30 x 30	40 x 40; 40 x 60; 60 x 60	40 x 60; 60 x 60; 36-inch drum	36 x 1,440
INPUT	Mediums				
	Magnetic Tape	No	Yes*	Yes	Yes*
	Punched Tape	No	Yes*	Yes	Yes*
	Punched Cards	No	Yes*	Yes	Yes*
	Manual Entry	No	Yes*	Yes	Yes*
	On-Line	Yes	Yes*	Yes	Yes*
	Codes	BCD	BCD	BCD	BCD
	On-Line Operation	—	—	—	—
OUTPUT	Maximum Speeds				
	Slewing (inches/sec)	20	10	10	25
	Writing (inches/sec)	10	10	10	25
	Resolution, inches	—	0.0005	0.0005	0.0005
	Repeatability, inches	0.003	0.001	0.001	0.001
	Accuracy, inches	0.015	±0.004	±0.004 (flatbed)	±0.004 (Y-axis)
	Number of Pens	1	1; 8*	1; 8*	1; 8*
	Plotting Modes	—	—	—	—
	Symbol Printing	Yes	Yes (62 characters)	Yes (62 characters)	Yes (62 characters)

PURCHASE PRICE, $	25,000	45,000	30,450	21,400
COMMENTS		Option: CRT Verifying Display	Option: CRT Verifying Display	Option: CRT Verifying Display

• Optional at extra cost

IDENTITY		Bolt Beranek and Newman Plotamatic Series 700 X-Y Recorders	Bolt Beranek and Newman Plotamatic Series 800 X-Y Recorders	Bolt Beranek and Newman Plotamatic Series 800A X-Y Recorders	Boston Digital N/CV 1105, N/CV 2905
REPORT NUMBER		—	—	—	—
TYPE		—	—	—	Drum
DRIVE SYSTEM		Servo	Servo	Servo	Stepper motors
USABLE PLOTTING AREA INCHES		7 x 10	10 x 15	10 x 15	11 x 120 (1105); 28.5 x 120 (2905)
INPUT	Mediums				
	Magnetic Tape	—	—	—	No
	Punched Tape	—	—	—	Yes (300 char/sec)
	Punched Cards	—	—	—	No
	Manual Entry	—	—	—	No
	On-Line	—	—	—	No
	Codes	—	—	—	9-channel EIA; ASCII*; Word address, var block Format: EIA RS-274A
	On-Line Operation	—	—	—	
OUTPUT	Maximum Speeds				
	Slewing (inches/sec)	15	30	20	—
	Writing (inches/sec)	15	20	20	90; 180
	Resolution, inches	<±0.1% full scale	<±0.1% full scale	<±0.1% full scale	0.005; 0.001
	Repeatability, inches	±0.1% full scale	±0.1%	±0.1%	See Comments
	Accuracy, inches	±0.2% full scale	±0.2% full scale	±0.15% full scale	± 1 increment
	Number of Pens	1	1	1	1
	Plotting Modes	Analog	Analog	Analog	1
	Symbol Printing	No	No	Yes (850)	None

PURCHASE PRICE, $	750 (705); 880 (715)	980 (815); 850 (805)	1,975 (800A); 1,795 (810A); 1,975 (850A)	16,775 (1105); 20,475 (2905)
COMMENTS	Model 705 is single range; Model 715 has 5 ranges/axis	Model 805 is single range; Model 815 has 5 ranges/axis	Model 800A has time base; Model 850A is point plotting system	Consists of Boston Digital adaptive unit and plotter made by another manufacturer; verifies N/C paper tape intended to control tool processing equipment; adapter enables plotter, linked to it by cable, to operate from tape punched in any code listed; specifications above are for these combinations: CalComp 565 (N/CV 1105), CalComp 563 (N/CV 2905); 1105 can be attached to Houston Instruments 6650 also; pairings with other plotters possible; circular interpolation optional

* Optional at extra cost

		CalComp 500 Series	CalComp 600 Series	CalComp 700 Series
IDENTITY		CalComp 500 Series	CalComp 600 Series	CalComp 700 Series
REPORT NUMBER		61.017.02	61.017.02	61.017.02
TYPE		Flatbed (502); drum (563, 565, 575)	Flatbed (602, 638); drum (663, 665)	Flatbed (702, 738); drum (763, 765)
DRIVE SYSTEM		Stepper motors	Stepper motors	Stepper motors
USABLE PLOTTING AREA INCHES		37 x 34 (502); 29.5 x 1,440 (563); 11 x 1,440 (565, 575)	31 x 34 (602); 48 x 72 (638); 29.5 x 1,440 (663); 11 x 1,440 (665)	31 x 34 (702); 48 x 72 (738); 48 x 60 (745); 29.5 x 1,440 (763); 11 x 1,440 (765)
INPUT	**Mediums**			
	Magnetic Tape	Yes*	Yes*	Yes*
	Punched Tape	Yes*	Yes*	Yes*
	Punched Cards	Yes*	Yes*	Yes*
	Manual Entry	—	—	—
	On-Line	Yes*	Yes*	Yes*
	Codes	—	—	—
	On-Line Operation	—	—	—
OUTPUT	**Maximum Speeds**			
	Slewing (inches/sec)	—	Same as writing	Same as writing
	Writing (inches/sec)	3 (502, 565); 2 (563)	2.25 (602); 1 (638); 3.5 (663); 4.5 (665)	9.3 (702); 4.6 (738); 13.1 (763); 16.9 (765); 4.2 (745)
	Resolution, inches	See Comments	0.001–0.010 (663, 665); 0.001–0.005 (602, 638)	0.001–0.005 (702); 0.0005, 0.001 (738); 0.001–0.10 (765, 763); 0.0001 (745)
	Repeatability, inches	—	—	0.0002 (745)
	Accuracy, inches	—	—	0.0012 (738); 0.0004 (745)
	Number of Pens	1	1 (602, 663, 665); 4 (638)	1 (702, 763, 765); 4 (738, 745)
	Plotting Modes	Incremental	Incremental	ZIP; incremental
	Symbol Printing	Yes	Yes	Yes

PURCHASE PRICE, $	Available from manufacturer; see report	Available from manufacturer; see report	Available from manufacturer; see report
COMMENTS	Resolution, inches: 0.005, 0.010 (565, 563); 0.010 (575); 0.01, 0.005, 0.002 (502)		

* Optional at extra cost

		CalComp 1136	Computervision INTERACTgraphic I Plotter/Digitizer	Concord Control Coordinatograph Plotting System	Concord Control Mark 8
IDENTITY					
REPORT NUMBER		61.017.02	—	—	—
TYPE		Drum	Flatbed	Flatbed	Flatbed
DRIVE SYSTEM		Stepper motors	Stepper motors	Servo	Servo
USABLE PLOTTING AREA INCHES		36.5 x 1,440	34 x 44; 34 x 56*	60 x 60	40 x 50
INPUT	Mediums				
	Magnetic Tape	Yes*	No	No	Yes*
	Punched Tape	Yes*	No	No	Yes*
	Punched Cards	Yes*	No	No	Yes*
	Manual Entry	—	Yes	No	Yes*
	On-Line	Yes*	Yes	Yes	No
	Codes	—	ASCII	—	—
	On-Line Operation	—	—	—	—
OUTPUT	Maximum Speeds				
	Slewing (inches/sec)	9.1	14	6	5
	Writing (inches/sec)	9.1	14	1	2
	Resolution, inches	0.0025	0.002	0.005	0.001
	Repeatability, inches	—	0.002	0.005	0.001
	Accuracy, inches	—	0.005	0.001	0.002
	Number of Pens	3	2	1	4
	Plotting Modes	Incremental	Long vector; short vector	—	—
	Symbol Printing	Yes	No	Yes	—

PURCHASE PRICE, $	Available from manufacturer	47,500	225,000	175,000 (includes PDP-8 computer, mag tape)
COMMENTS		CRT display is integral part of system (see Graphic Displays comparison charts); system can function as digitizer	Photo-projection head available	System operates as on-line interactive plotter/digitizer

• Optional at extra cost

		Dresser Systems LGP-2000	Electronic Associates 430/100	Electronic Associates 130, 230	Electronic Associates 135
IDENTITY		Dresser Systems LGP-2000	Electronic Associates 430/100	Electronic Associates 130, 230	Electronic Associates 135
REPORT NUMBER		61.129.01	—	—	—
TYPE		Electro-optical	Flatbed	Flatbed	Flatbed
DRIVE SYSTEM		Stepper motors	Servo; digitally controlled	Incremental	Incremental
USABLE PLOTTING AREA INCHES		40 x 1,200	31 x 36	11 x 1,728	11 x 1,728
INPUT	Mediums				
	Magnetic Tape	Yes	Yes*	No	No
	Punched Tape	No	Yes*	No	No
	Punched Cards	No	No	No	No
	Manual Entry	No	No	No	No
	On-Line	Yes	Yes*	Yes	Yes
	Codes	—	—	6 bits	4 or 6 bits
	On-Line Operation	—	—	Yes	Yes
OUTPUT	Maximum Speeds				
	Slewing (inches/sec)	1,520 sq. inches/min	24	3.0 (130); 2.7 (230)	3.0
	Writing (inches/sec)	1,520 sq. inches/min	16	3.0 (130); 2.7 (230)	3.0
	Resolution, inches	0.01; 0.005	0.001	0.010; 0.005*	0.010; 0.005*
	Repeatability, inches	0.001	0.003	—	—
	Accuracy, inches	0.005	—	—	—
	Number of Pens	—	1; 4*; 8*	1	1
	Plotting Modes	—	Point; line; free scribe; rapid	Incremental	Incremental
	Symbol Printing	No	Yes*	By software	By software

PURCHASE PRICE, $	91,000 (on-line) to 176,000 (off-line)	32,800 (on-line); 47,500 (off-line)	3,450 (130); 6,250 (230)	3,650
COMMENTS	Uses laser light source to produce images on photographic film	Automatic velocity control, automatic error detection, and linear interpolation std	230 (remote version of 130) specifies improved rates for remote plotting (accomplished by data compression technique)	

* Optional at extra cost

IDENTITY		Electronic Associates 140	Electronic Associates 145	Electronic Associates 430/200	
REPORT NUMBER		—	—	—	
TYPE		Flatbed	Flatbed	Flatbed	
DRIVE SYSTEM		Incremental	Incremental	Servo; digitally controlled	
USABLE PLOTTING AREA INCHES		11 x 1,728	11 x 1,728	54 x 76	
INPUT	Mediums				
	Magnetic Tape	No	No	Yes*	
	Punched Tape	No	No	Yes*	
	Punched Cards	No	No	No	
	Manual Entry	No	No	No	
	On-Line	Yes	Yes	Yes*	
	Codes	6 bits	4 or 6 bits	—	
	On-Line Operation	Yes	Yes	—	
OUTPUT	Maximum Speeds				
	Slewing (inches/sec)	2.25	2.25	16	
	Writing (inches/sec)	2.25	2.25	12	
	Resolution, inches	0.005	0.005	0.00125	
	Repeatability, inches	—	—	0.004	
	Accuracy, inches	—	—	—	
	Number of Pens	1	1	1; 4*; 8*	
	Plotting Modes	Incremental	Incremental	Point; line; free scribe; rapid	
	Symbol Printing	By software	By software	Yes*	

PURCHASE PRICE, $	3,450	4,150	54,300 (on-line); 69,000 (off-line)	
COMMENTS				

* Optional at extra cost

	IDENTITY	Electronic Associates 3500 Series		Faul-Coradi Coradomat 21	Geo Space DP-203
	REPORT NUMBER	—	—	—	—
	TYPE	Flatbed	Flatbed	Flatbed	CRT on photosensitive material
	DRIVE SYSTEM	Servo	Servo	Servo	Drum
	USABLE PLOTTING AREA INCHES	30 x 30	45 x 60	51 x 63	40 x 60
INPUT	Mediums				
	Magnetic Tape	Yes*	Yes*	Yes*	Yes
	Punched Tape	Yes	Yes	Yes*	No
	Punched Cards	Yes	Yes	Yes*	Yes
	Manual Entry	Yes	Yes	Yes*	No
	On-Line	Yes*	Yes*	—	Yes
	Codes	—	—	All	—
	On-Line Operation	—	—	—	—
OUTPUT	Maximum Speeds				
	Slewing (inches/sec)	30	20	2	4 x 10-inch area/sec
	Writing (inches/sec)	15	10	2	40 x 60-inch area/sec
	Resolution, inches	0.002	0.002	0.0004	0.005; 0.010
	Repeatability, inches	0.003	0.006	0.0008	0.0025; 0.005
	Accuracy, inches	0.015	0.030 (X); 0.022 (Y)	0.0015	0.0015
	Number of Pens	1; 8*	1; 8*	1; 5*	—
	Plotting Modes	Point; line; free scribe	Point; line; free scribe	Absolute; incremental	—
	Symbol Printing	Yes*	Yes*	Yes*	Yes

PURCHASE PRICE, $	19,800 (card input); 37,550 (mag tape)	26,950 (card input); 44,700 (mag tape)	96,000	37,000 (on-line); 130,000 (off-line)
COMMENTS	No longer marketed	No longer marketed	No longer marketed	

* Optional at extra cost

		Gerber 22 Table	Gerber 26 Table	Gerber 32 Table	Gerber 33 Table
IDENTITY		Gerber 22 Table	Gerber 26 Table	Gerber 32 Table	Gerber 33 Table
REPORT NUMBER		61.047.01	61.047.01	61.047.01	61.047.01
TYPE		Flatbed	Flatbed	Flatbed	Flatbed
DRIVE SYSTEM		Stepper motors	Stepper motors	Stepper motors	Stepper motors
USABLE PLOTTING AREA INCHES		48 x 58	34 x 44	48 x 60	24 x 24
INPUT	Mediums				
	Magnetic Tape	Yes*	Yes*	Yes*	Yes*
	Punched Tape	Yes	Yes	Yes*	Yes*
	Punched Cards	Yes*	Yes*	Yes*	Yes*
	Manual Entry	Yes	Yes	Yes*	Yes*
	On-Line	Yes*	Yes*	Yes*	Yes*
	Codes	EIA; ASCII	EIA; ASCII	EIA; ASCII	EIA; ASCII
	On-Line Operation	—	—	—	—
OUTPUT	Maximum Speeds				
	Slewing (inches/sec)	10	10	1	1
	Writing (inches/sec)	10	10	1	1
	Resolution, inches	0.001	0.001	0.0001	0.0001
	Repeatability, inches	0.003	0.0025	0.0005	0.0002
	Accuracy, inches	0.005	0.004	0.0009	0.0005
	Number of Pens	1; 2*; 3*; 6*	1; 2*; 3*; 6*	1; 6*	1; 6*
	Plotting Modes	Absolute; incremental	Absolute; incremental	Absolute; incremental	Absolute; incremental
	Symbol Printing	Yes	Yes	Yes	Yes

PURCHASE PRICE, $	70,000 (including Series 700 Control)	66,000 (including Series 700 Control)	143,000 (including Series 700 Control)	143,000 (including Series 700 Control)
COMMENTS	Can be used with any Gerber controller	Can be used with any Gerber controller	Can be used with any Gerber controller	Can be used with any Gerber controller

* Optional at extra cost

	IDENTITY	Gerber 75 Table	Gerber 62 Drum Plotter	Gerber 82 Electrographic Plotter	Gerber System 40
	REPORT NUMBER	61.047.01	—	—	61.047.01
	TYPE	Flatbed	Drum	Electrographic	Flatbed
	DRIVE SYSTEM	Stepper motors	Servo; digitally controlled	Servo; digitally controlled	Stepper motors
	USABLE PLOTTING AREA INCHES	60 x 96 to 72 x 288	36 x 1,500	9 x 14	14 x 20
INPUT	Mediums				
	Magnetic Tape	Yes*	Yes	Yes	Yes*
	Punched Tape	Yes	Yes	Yes	Yes*
	Punched Cards	Yes*	Yes	Yes	Yes*
	Manual Entry	Yes	Yes	Yes	Yes*
	On-Line	Yes*	Yes	Yes	Yes*
	Codes	EIA; ASCII	—	—	EIA; ASCII
	On-Line Operation	—	—	—	—
OUTPUT	Maximum Speeds				
	Slewing (inches/sec)	10	1,200	Automatic sheet feed	2.4
	Writing (inches/sec)	10	1,200 (axial)	1,200 (axial)	2.4
	Resolution, inches	0.001	±0.002	±0.002	0.0005
	Repeatability, inches	0.002	±0.005	Not available	0.0005
	Accuracy, inches	0.005	±0.010	Not available	0.001
	Number of Pens	1; 6*	4	1	1
	Plotting Modes	Absolute; incremental	1	1	—
	Symbol Printing	Yes	By controller software	By controller software	Yes

PURCHASE PRICE, $	92,000 (including Series 700 Control)	27,500 (approx)	18,000 (approx)	35,000
COMMENTS	Can be used with any Gerber controller	Can be used with any Gerber controller; Series 400 Controller, developed for Model 62, uses mag tape input	Can be used with any Gerber controller; will plot solid black areas	

* Optional at extra cost

	IDENTITY	Graphic Data 71B	Hewlett-Packard 7200A	Houston Instrument COMPLOT DP-1	Houston Instrument COMPLOT DP-3
	REPORT NUMBER	—	—	61.054.01	61.054.01
	TYPE	Electrographic	Electromechanical	Drum	Drum
	DRIVE SYSTEM	Stepper motors	—	Stepper motors	Stepper motors
	USABLE PLOTTING AREA INCHES	11 x 17	11 x 17	11 x 1,728	22 x 1,728
INPUT	Mediums				
	Magnetic Tape	Yes	—	Yes*	Yes*
	Punched Tape	No	Yes, from TTY	No	No
	Punched Cards	No	—	No	No
	Manual Entry	No	Yes	No	No
	On-Line	Yes	Yes	Yes*	Yes*
	Codes	—	ASCII	—	—
	On-Line Operation	—	—	Yes*	Yes*
OUTPUT	Maximum Speeds				
	Slewing (inches/sec)	—	—	4.2	4.2
	Writing (inches/sec)	4	1.1 sec/point, line	4.2	4.2
	Resolution, inches	0.010	0.005	0.005; 0.010	0.005; 0.010
	Repeatability, inches	0.003	0.007	0.005; 0.010	0.005; 0.010
	Accuracy, inches	0.005	0.03	0.005; 0.010	0.005; 0.010
	Number of Pens	100 writing elements	1	1	1
	Plotting Modes	Asynchronous	Point; line	Incremental	Incremental
	Symbol Printing	Yes	No	No	No

PURCHASE PRICE, $	15,000–25,000	3,300 Lease: 145/mo Rent: 200/mo	3,550	6,400
COMMENTS		Absolute coordinates; draws vectors in any direction, up to 3 inches long	Step sizes of 0.10 mm, 0.25 mm available on request	Step sizes of 0.10 mm, 0.25 mm available on request

* Optional at extra cost

IDENTITY		Houston Instrument COMPLOT DP-5	Houston Instrument COMPLOT DP-12	I/O Systems Transplotter	
REPORT NUMBER		61.054.01	61.054.01	—	
TYPE		Drum	Drum	—	
DRIVE SYSTEM		Stepper motors	Stepper motors	—	
USABLE PLOTTING AREA INCHES		11 x 1,728	11 x 1,728	11 x 17	
INPUT	Mediums				
	Magnetic Tape	Yes*	No	Yes	
	Punched Tape	No	No	Yes	
	Punched Cards	No	No	Yes	
	Manual Entry	No	No	Yes	
	On-Line	Yes*	Yes (remote)	Yes	
	Codes	—	—	ASCII; EBCDIC; EIA	
	On-Line Operation	Yes*	Yes (remote)	Yes	
OUTPUT	Maximum Speeds				
	Slewing (inches/sec)	8.4	4.2	30	
	Writing (inches/sec)	8.4	4.2	15	
	Resolution, inches	0.0025; 0.005	0.005; 0.010	0.005	
	Repeatability, inches	0.0025; 0.005	0.005; 0.010	0.01	
	Accuracy, inches	0.0025; 0.005	0.005; 0.010	0.1	
	Number of Pens	1	1	1	
	Plotting Modes	Incremental	Incremental	Point; continuous	
	Symbol Printing	No	No	Via software	

PURCHASE PRICE, $	11,000	4,550	3,200 complete; 2,200 without plotter	
COMMENTS		Step sizes of 0.10 mm, 0.25 mm available on request		

* **Optional at extra cost**

IDENTITY		Kongsberg Systems Kingmatic 1215, 1800, 2637	Mergenthaler Diagrammer D4TM Automatic Plotter & Artwork Generator	Mergenthaler Diagrammer D5TT Automatic Plotter, Digitizer & Artwork Generator
REPORT NUMBER		—	—	—
TYPE		—	Vertical flatbed	Vertical flatbed
DRIVE SYSTEM		—	Stepper motors	Stepper motors
USABLE PLOTTING AREA INCHES		48 x 60 (1215); 72 x 60–420 (1800); 96 x 144 (2637)	28 x 40	28 x 40
INPUT	**Mediums**			
	Magnetic Tape	Yes	No	No
	Punched Tape	Yes	Yes	Yes
	Punched Cards	Yes	No	No
	Manual Entry	Yes	Yes	Yes
	On-Line	Yes	No	No
	Codes	EIA; ASCII; ISO	EIA	EIA
	On-Line Operation	—	—	—
OUTPUT	**Maximum Speeds**			
	Slewing (inches/sec)	—	6	6
	Writing (inches/sec)	6.7 (1215); 10 (1800, 2637)	—	—
	Resolution, inches	0.00025–0.002 (selectable)	0.025	0.025
	Repeatability, inches	0.0004 (1215); 0.0008 (1800, 2637)	±0.0005	±0.0005
	Accuracy, inches	0.001 (1215); 0.0002 (1800, 2637)	0.003	0.003
	Number of Pens	4	—	—
	Plotting Modes	Absolute; incremental	—	—
	Symbol Printing	—	Yes	Yes

PURCHASE PRICE, $	60,000-100,000 (1215); 125,000-200,000 (1800); 135,000-160,000 (2637)	55,900	70,150
COMMENTS	Optical writing head	Also available in semi-automatic models priced from $34,900; photo-projection head only; 256 symbols (up to 3 inches in diameter) from library of over 10,000	System operates as an on-line interactive plotter digitizer; photo-projection head only; 256 symbols (up to 3 inches in diameter) from library of over 10,000

	IDENTITY	Milgo DPS-7	Omega-T Systems Fast Plot	Perspective Systems Recordomat 1250-2
	REPORT NUMBER	—	—	—
	TYPE	Flatbed	—	—
	DRIVE SYSTEM	Servo	—	—
	USABLE PLOTTING AREA INCHES	30 x 30 (4021 DM-1); 44 x 60 (4021 DM-2); 30 x 30 (4021 DM-1); 44 x 60 (4021 DM-12)	11 x 17	30 x 40
INPUT	Mediums			
	Magnetic Tape	Yes	No	Yes
	Punched Tape	No	Yes	No
	Punched Cards	No	No	No
	Manual Entry	No	No	Yes
	On-Line	Yes*	Yes	Yes
	Codes	—	ASCII	BCD; EBCDIC
	On-Line Operation	—	—	—
OUTPUT	Maximum Speeds			
	Slewing (inches/sec)	4.8 (4021 DM-1, DM-2); 12 (4021 DM-11, DM-12)	10	20
	Writing (inches/sec)	4.8 (4021 DM-1, DM-2); 20 (4021 DM-11, DM-12)	10	3.2
	Resolution, inches	0.004	0.01	0.005
	Repeatability, inches	0.003 (4021 DM-1, DM-11) 0.006 (X); 0.005 (Y) (4021 DM-2, DM-12)	0.05	0.005
	Accuracy, inches	0.015 (4021 DM-1, DM-11) 0.030 (X); 0.022 (Y) (4021 DM-2, DM-12)	—	—
	Number of Pens	2	1	2
	Plotting Modes	Incremental	—	—
	Symbol Printing	Via software	Yes	No

PURCHASE PRICE, $	40,000 (4021 DM-1); 45,000 (2021 DM-2); 44,000 (4021 DM-11); 51,000 (4021 DM-12)	3,500	84,000
COMMENTS			Can also be used as a digitizer

• Optional at extra cost

IDENTITY		Spatial Data Systems 501-3	Time Share Peripherals TSP-212 Plotting System	Time Share Peripherals TSP-12 Plotter Controller	
REPORT NUMBER		—	—	—	
TYPE		Electromechanical	—	—	
DRIVE SYSTEM		Stepper motors	Analog plotting system	Analog plotting system	
USABLE PLOTTING AREA INCHES		11 x 17 x 3 (see Comments)	11 x 15	—	
INPUT	**Mediums**				
	Magnetic Tape	Yes			
	Punched Tape	Yes			
	Punched Cards	No			
	Manual Entry	No	Yes (in some cases)	Yes (in some cases)	
	On-Line	Yes	Yes	Yes	
	Codes	—	ASCII; IBM Correspondence; IBM BCD	ASCII; IBM Correspondence; IBM BCD	
	On-Line Operation	—	Yes	Yes	
OUTPUT	**Maximum Speeds**				
	Slewing (inches/sec)	300 steps/sec	150 to 400 points/min depending upon system used	150 to 400 points/min depending upon system used	
	Writing (inches/sec)	120 points/min			
	Resolution, inches	0.01	0.2% of full scale	1/512 of full scale	
	Repeatability, inches	0.01	—	—	
	Accuracy, inches	0.05	±0.2% of full scale	1/256 of full scale	
	Number of Pens	—	1	1	
	Plotting Modes	Point	—	—	
	Symbol Printing	No	Via software	Via software	

PURCHASE PRICE, $	23,500	3,300	—	
COMMENTS	Steel wires fixed in plotting table produce 3-D representation	Used as time sharing plotter	Time sharing plotter controller will drive most standard X-Y recorders as output device	

IDENTITY		Tridea Electronics Aldraft Series			Unitech AristoGraph System 201
REPORT NUMBER		—			—
TYPE		Flatbed (optional level or tiltable configurations)			Flatbed
DRIVE SYSTEM		Servo			Stepper motors
USABLE PLOTTING AREA INCHES		60 x 48–60 x 72	60 x 72–60 x 168	60 x 168–60 x 288	48 x 60
INPUT	**Mediums**				
	Magnetic Tape	7-, 9-track*			Yes*
	Punched Tape	Yes			Yes (8 channels)
	Punched Cards	No			No
	Manual Entry	Teletype ASR 33			Teletype ASR 33
	On-Line	No			No
	Codes	EIA RS-244; ASCII (paper tape) BCD			EIA RS-244A; ASCII
	On-Line Operation	Format: word address or tab sequential; EIA RS-274A			Format: EIA RS-274B
OUTPUT	**Maximum Speeds**				
	Slewing (inches/sec)	300	600	600	480; 960*
	Writing (inches/sec)	8.33	8.33	8.33	Up to 480; 960*
	Resolution, inches	0.010	0.010	0.010	0.001; 0.002 for higher writing option
	Repeatability, inches	±0.001	±0.002	±0.0025	±0.001
	Accuracy, inches	±0.002	±0.004	±0.005	±0.002
	Number of Pens	6	6	6	4 (also has rotatable head for cutting)
	Plotting Modes	Continuous tracing (automatic and manual); "point-picking"	Continuous tracing (automatic and manual); "point-picking"	Continuous tracing (automatic and manual); "point-picking"	Normal drafting mode
	Symbol Printing	Alphanumeric software package; special symbols also available	Alphanumeric software package; special symbols also available	Alphanumeric software package; special symbols also available	Yes (under software control, as specified by input tape or ASR 33)

PURCHASE PRICE, $	150,000–200,000	74,750
COMMENTS	Uses Varian 620/i, 8K memory, 16-bit word length, optional memory to 32K; vacuum holddown 10 inches mercury; system developed for N/C tape	Multipurpose drawing capabilities; internal processor: PDP 8/L; vacuum hold-down; 2-axis, 6-digit coordinate readout* (sometimes used as position indicator); software control: linear, circular, parabolic interpolation; alphanumerics; axis selection and inversion; scaling perspective, etc.

* Optional at extra cost

IDENTITY		Unitech Aristo 4416 Coordinatograph	Unitech Aristo 4440 Coordinatograph	Unitech Aristo 4441 Coordinatograph	
REPORT NUMBER		—	—	—	
TYPE		Manual (see Comments)	Manual (see Comments)	Manual (see Comments)	
DRIVE SYSTEM		Manual	Manual	Manual	
USABLE PLOTTING AREA INCHES		26 x 39	33 x 43	47 x 51	
INPUT	Mediums Magnetic Tape Punched Tape Punched Cards Manual Entry On-Line	Operator reads dials or optionally supplied digital display of coordinates	Operator reads dials or optionally supplied digital display of coordinates	Operator reads dials or optionally supplied digital display of coordinates	
	Codes	—	—	—	
	On-Line Operation	—	—	—	
OUTPUT	Maximum Speeds Slewing (inches/sec) Writing (inches/sec)	—	—	—	
	Resolution, inches	0.001	0.0005	0.0005	
	Repeatability, inches	0.0015	0.0004	0.0004	
	Accuracy, inches	±0.003 (with std scales); ±0.002 (digital readout)	±0.0008	±0.0008	
	Number of Pens	3 (scribes, chisel, double-line pen; see Comments)	1 tool at a time (pen or scribe)	1 tool at a time (pen or scribe)	
	Plotting Modes	—	—	—	
	Symbol Printing	—	—	—	

<table>
<tr><td>PURCHASE PRICE, $</td><td>2,500</td><td>8,500</td><td>9,350</td><td></td></tr>
<tr><td rowspan="2">COMMENTS</td><td rowspan="2">Used singly; manual drafting system that cannot be automated; occasionally used as inexpensive digitizer with aid of added electronics</td><td>Manual drafting system that can be automated with certain accessories; digital readout capability* permits use as digitizer with proper accessories</td><td>Manual drafting system that can be automated with certain accessories; digital readout capability* permits use as digitizer with proper accessories</td><td rowspan="2"></td></tr>
<tr><td colspan="2">Plotters are equipped with the following scale combinations for industrial use:
10" = 1", 20" = 1", 25" = 1", 50" = 1"
For surveying:
1" = 100', 1" = 200', 1" = 400', 1" = 500'
Other scales can be provided at extra cost; drafts with pencil or ink; engraves on coated plastic foil, glass plates, or sheet metal; used extensively for automatic tool- and die-making processes and for making IC masks; can also verify N/C tapes</td></tr>
</table>

* Optional at extra cost

		Unitech Aristo 4446 Coordinatograph	Unitech Aristo 4448 Coordinatograph	Unitech Optimat	Universal Drafting Machine Orthomat 4000
IDENTITY		Unitech Aristo 4446 Coordinatograph	Unitech Aristo 4448 Coordinatograph	Unitech Optimat	Universal Drafting Machine Orthomat 4000
REPORT NUMBER		—	—	—	—
TYPE		Manual (see Comments)	Manual (see Comments)	Flatbed	Flatbed
DRIVE SYSTEM		Manual	Manual	Stepper motors	Stepper motors
USABLE PLOTTING AREA INCHES		47 x 59	59 x 79	33 x 43–47 x 59	48 x 72
INPUT	Mediums	Operator reads dials or optionally supplied digital display of coordinates	Operator reads dials or optionally supplied digital display of coordinates		
	Magnetic Tape			Yes*	Yes*
	Punched Tape			Yes	Yes*
	Punched Cards			No	Yes*
	Manual Entry			Yes	Yes*
	On-Line			No	Yes*
	Codes	—	—	Special Optimat code (compacted binary)	—
	On-Line Operation	—	—	No	—
OUTPUT	Maximum Speeds	—	—		
	Slewing (inches/sec)			Up to 170 or 340*	6.6
	Writing (inches/sec)			Up to 170 or 340*	6.6
	Resolution, inches	0.0006	0.0006	0.0005; 0.001	0.001
	Repeatability, inches	0.0005	0.0005	±0.0006; ±0.0008	0.001
	Accuracy, inches	±0.0012	±0.0012	±0.001; ±0.0015	0.006
	Number of Pens	1 tool at a time	1 tool at a time	Rotatable knife; 1 pen*	6; 4; 1
	Plotting Modes	—	—	Normal drawing mode	—
	Symbol Printing	—	—	No	—

PURCHASE PRICE, $	12,400	14.900	47,000	70,000 (includes PDP-8 computer)
COMMENTS	Manual drafting system that can be automated with certain accessories	Manual drafting system that cannot be automated	Intended primarily for cutting a rubylith; internal processor: PDP 8/L; also has Teletype ASR 33 high-speed punch*; based in some respects on Aristo 4440, 4441, and 4446	
	Digital readout capability* permits use as digitizer with proper accessories; available scales are the same as those given for Aristo 4440 and 4441; drafts with pencil or ink; engraves on coated plastic foil, glass plates, or sheet metal; used extensively for automatic tool- and die-making processes and for making IC masks; can also verify N/C tapes	(spans with preceding column)		

* Optional at extra cost

IDENTITY		Universal Drafting Machine Orthomat 5000	University Computing 300 Series	University Computing 1430 Series	University Computing 2000 Series
REPORT NUMBER		—	61.023.02	61.023.02	61.023.02
TYPE		Flatbed	Drum	Drum	Drum
DRIVE SYSTEM		Servo	Stepper motor	Stepper motor	Stepper motor
USABLE PLOTTING AREA INCHES		60 x 96; up to 72 x 288	29 x 1,220; 10.5 x 1,220	13 x 1,920	29 x 1,920; 10.5 x 1,920
INPUT	**Mediums**				
	Magnetic Tape	Yes*	Yes*	No	Yes*
	Punched Tape	Yes*	Yes*	No	Yes*
	Punched Cards	Yes*	Yes*	No	Yes*
	Manual Entry	Yes*	No	No	No
	On-Line	Yes*	Yes	Yes	Yes
	Codes	—	UCC format	UCC format	UCC format
	On-Line Operation	—	—	—	—
OUTPUT	**Maximum Speeds**				
	Slewing (inches/sec)	6.6	2.8; 4.2	2.1; 3.5	7.07
	Writing (inches/sec)	6.6	2.8; 4.2	2.1; 3.5	7.07
	Resolution, inches	0.001	0.005; 0.010	0.005; 0.010	0.0025
	Repeatability, inches	0.001	0.005; 0.010	0.005; 0.010	0.0025
	Accuracy, inches	0.005	±0.005, ±0.010 (X axis); ±0.65% (Y axis)	±0.005, ±0.010 (X axis); ±0.65% (Y axis)	±0.0025 (X axis); ±0.13% (Y axis)
	Number of Pens	6	1	1	1
	Plotting Modes	—	Incremental (selectable); Delta (see Comments)	Incremental	Incremental (variable under program control); Delta
	Symbol Printing	—	Software controlled	Software controlled	Software controlled

PURCHASE PRICE, $	125,000 (includes PDP-8 computer)	7,750 (on-line); 29,250 (off-line via mag tape)	4,300	16,500 (on-line); 47,750 (off-line via mag tape)
COMMENTS	Digitizing available as optional feature	Delta control allows block transfer of data (127 increments/command); compatible with principal computers; 12-inch paper adapter*; operator choice of paper takeup or spillout; 0.005 step size: 400 step/sec operation; 0.010 step size: 300 step/sec operation; pen-point exposure for manual setting of origin	Selectable step sizes of 0.010 inch, 0.005 inch, 0.2mm or 0.1mm set at factory; compatible with principal computers; compatible with Cope and Datel terminals	Programmable speed control of 2,000, 1,600, 1,200, or 800 steps/sec (7.07 inches/sec max); 12-inch paper adapter*; compatible with principal computers; compatible with Cope terminals; Delta control allows block transfer of data (1,023 increments/command)

* Optional at extra cost

		Varian STATOS-5 Model 500	Varian STATOS-5 Model 514	Xynetics 500	Xynetics 1100
IDENTITY		Varian STATOS-5 Model 500	Varian STATOS-5 Model 514	Xynetics 500	Xynetics 1100
REPORT NUMBER		—	—	61.132.01	61.132.01
TYPE		Electrostatic printer/plotter	Electrostatic printer/plotter	Flatbed	Flatbed
DRIVE SYSTEM		Stepper motors	Stepper motors	See Comments	See Comments
USABLE PLOTTING AREA INCHES		12.8 by indefinite roll feed	14 by indefinite roll feed	48 x 64	48 x 64
INPUT	Mediums				
	Magnetic Tape	Yes	Yes	Yes	Yes
	Punched Tape	—	—	Yes	Yes
	Punched Cards	—	—	Yes	Yes
	Manual Entry	—	—	Yes	Yes
	On-Line	Yes	Yes	Yes	Yes
	Codes	Binary; BCD; ASCII	Binary; BCD; ASCII	—	—
	On-Line Operation	—	—	—	—
OUTPUT	Maximum Speeds				
	Slewing (inches/sec)	—	—	40	40
	Writing (inches/sec)	51 sq. inches/sec	56 sq. inches/sec	40	40
	Resolution, inches	0.005	0.005	0.001	0.001
	Repeatability, inches	—	—	0.001	0.001
	Accuracy, inches	—	—	0.005	0.005
	Number of Pens	1,024 styli across chart width	1,400 styli across chart width	4	4
	Plotting Modes	—	—	—	—
	Symbol Printing	Yes	Yes	Yes	Yes

PURCHASE PRICE, $	14,900	18,500	19,000 (table only)	33,000 (table only)
COMMENTS			Sawyer Principle drive; electromagnets in plotting head interact with fixed grid of magnetic material to produce movement	Sawyer Principle drive; electromagnets in plotting head interact with fixed grid of magnetic material to produce movement

* Optional at extra cost

	IDENTITY	Xynetics 1200	Zeta Research 130	Zeta Research 145	Zeta Research 230
	REPORT NUMBER	61.132.01	—	—	—
	TYPE	Flatbed	Flatbed	Flatbed	Flatbed
	DRIVE SYSTEM	See Comments	Stepper motors	Stepper motors	Stepper motors
	USABLE PLOTTING AREA INCHES	64 x 96	11 x 1,728	11 x 1,728	11 x 1,728
INPUT	Mediums				
	Magnetic Tape	Yes	No	No	No
	Punched Tape	Yes	No	No	No
	Punched Cards	Yes	No	No	No
	Manual Entry	Yes	Yes	Yes	Yes
	On-Line	Yes	Yes	Yes	Yes
	Codes	—	—	—	—
	On-Line Operation	—	—	—	—
OUTPUT	Maximum Speeds				
	Slewing (inches/sec)	40	—	—	—
	Writing (inches/sec)	40	3	2.25	2.7
	Resolution, inches	0.001	0.010	0.005	0.010
	Repeatability, inches	0.001	0.005	0.0025	0.005
	Accuracy, inches	0.005	—	—	—
	Number of Pens	4	1	1; 2	1; 2
	Plotting Modes	—	—	—	—
	Symbol Printing	Yes	No	No	No

PURCHASE PRICE, $	53,000 (table only)	3,450	4,150	6,250
COMMENTS	Sawyer Principle drive; electromagnets in plotting head interact with fixed grid of magnetic material to produce movement			

* Optional at extra cost

APPENDIX III: COMPARISON CHARTS: IMAGE DIGITIZERS

The charts on the following pages present summary characteristics of currently available image digitizers. The Report Number entry in the charts indexes complete device coverage in *AUERBACH Graphic Processing Reports.*

IDENTITY		Auto-trol 3400	Auto-trol 3700	Auto-trol 3800/B, A	Bendix Datagrid Digitizer
REPORT NUMBER		—	—	41.009.01	41.114.01
TYPE		Electromechanical	Electromechanical	Electromechanical	All electronic
USABLE DIGITIZING AREA, inches		24 x 36; 36 x 48	20 x 20 to 60 x 80 in even inch increments	40 x 60; 48 x 60 (std); up to 60 x 80 inches	30 x 36; 36 x 48; 42 x 60
INPUT	Cursor	Yes	Yes	Yes	Yes
	Keyboard	Yes	Yes	Yes	Yes
	Other	No	No	No	Thumbwheel switches
OUTPUT	Mediums				
	Magnetic Tape	Yes	Yes	Yes	Yes
	Paper Tape	Yes	Yes	Yes	Yes
	Punched Cards	Yes	Yes	Yes	Yes
	On-Line	Yes	Yes	Yes	Yes
	Other	Printer	Printer	Printer	Teletype
	Format Control Patch Panel	Yes	Yes	Yes	Yes
	Other	No	No	No	No

CHARACTERISTICS	Max Speed, inches/sec	2,000 inches/min	100	100	300
	Resolution, inches	0.001	0.001	0.001	0.001
	Accuracy, inches	0.004	0.004	0.004	0.005
	Digitizing Modes	Absolute; incremental; point	Absolute	Absolute; incremental (3800 A)	Absolute; incremental
	Scaling	Yes	Yes	Yes*	Yes
	Grid Roundoff	No	No	Yes (3800A)	Yes
	Other	No	No	No	Yes (rotation)
MINIMUM PRICE, $		15,500	9,450 + 4,700 for table	15,850 (3800B); 19,250 (3800A)	16,965
COMMENTS					

* Optional

		Bolt Beranek and Newman Grafacon 1010A	Bolt Beranek and Newman Grafacon 2020	Data Tech APD	Instronics Gradicon Graphic Coordinate Digitizer
IDENTITY					
REPORT NUMBER		—	—	41.030.01	41.133.01
TYPE		Tablet	Tablet	Electromechanical	Electromechanical servo
USABLE DIGITIZING AREA, inches		10.24 x 10.24	20:48 x 20.48	26 x 36; 36 x 46	24 x 36; 36 x 48; 48 x 60
INPUT	Cursor	No	No	Yes	Yes
	Keyboard	No	No	Yes	Yes
	Other	Stylus pen	Pen-like stylus	Thumbwheel switches	Switches
OUTPUT	Mediums Magnetic Tape	Yes*	Yes*	Yes*	Yes
	Paper Tape	Yes*	Yes*	Yes	Yes
	Punched Cards	Yes*	Yes*	Yes*	Yes
	On-Line	Yes	Yes	No	Yes
	Other	Plotter*; CRT*	Plotter*; CRT*	Teletypewriter; printer	Typewriter
	Format Control Patch Panel	— —	— —	—	Yes
	Other	—	—	See Comments	—

CHARACTERISTICS	Max Speed, inches/sec	45	90	50	16
	Resolution, inches	0.01; 0.02; 0.04	0.02	0.001	0.001
	Accuracy, inches	0.01; 0.02; 0.04	0.02	0.001	0.004
	Digitizing Modes	Point; continuous	Point; continuous	Absolute; incremental	Absolute; incremental
	Scaling	—	—	Yes	Yes
	Grid Roundoff	—	—	Yes	Yes
	Other	—	—		—
MINIMUM PRICE, $		4,950	12,500	13,900	15,300
COMMENTS		Film projection optionally available	Film projection optionally available	System is hardwired and tailored specifically to the user's requirements; another model, the UPD, has general-purpose minicomputer for format control	

• Optional

	IDENTITY	Edwin Industries Pencil Follower	Faul-Coradi Coradigraph	Faul-Coradi DigiRail Digitizer	Gerber GCD-1
	REPORT NUMBER	—	—	—	41.3995.010
	TYPE	—	Electromechanical	Electromechanical	—
	USABLE DIGITIZING AREA, inches	24 x 36; 36 x 48; 48 x 60	20 x 20 to 80 x 60	54 x 40	42 x 60
INPUT	Cursor	Yes	Yes	Yes	Yes
	Keyboard	Yes	Yes	Yes	Yes
	Other	Thumbwheel switches	Footswitch	Footswitch	Fixed data switches
OUTPUT	Mediums				
	Magnetic Tape	Yes	Yes*	Yes*	Yes*
	Paper Tape	Yes	Yes	Yes	Yes*
	Punched Cards	Yes	Yes*	Yes*	Yes
	On-Line	Yes	No	No	Yes*
	Other	Typewriter	—	—	—
	Format Control Patch Panel	Yes	Yes	Yes	Yes
	Other	—	No	No	—

CHARACTERISTICS	Max Speed, inches/sec	20	25	100	—
	Resolution, inches	0.001	0.001; 0.0001	0.001	0.001
	Accuracy, inches	0.004	0.0015; 0.0008	0.005	0.010
	Digitizing Modes	Absolute; incremental	Absolute; incremental	Absolute; incremental	Absolute; incremental
	Scaling	—	Yes	Yes	Yes*
	Grid Roundoff	Yes	Yes	Yes	Yes*
	Other	—	Preset in X and Y	Preset in X and Y	—
MINIMUM PRICE, $		10,800	20,000	20,000	13,900
COMMENTS		Film projection is also available No longer marketed	Repeatability is 0.0004 with 0.0001 resolution and 0.0001 with 0.001 resolution No longer marketed	No longer marketed	

* Optional

IDENTITY		Boston Digital LTD/1	Concord Control Graphic Data Digitizer	Concord Control Universal Graphics Processor Mark 8	Unitech Programming System 23
REPORT NUMBER					
TYPE		Electromechanical (flat table)	Electromechanical (flat table)	Servo	Electromechanical (drafting table)
USABLE DIGITIZING AREA, inches		22 x 34 (accepts D-size drawings)	22 x 32	40 x 50	42 x 60
INPUT	**Cursor**	Yes	Yes	Yes	Yes (armless)
	Keyboard	Yes (9)	Yes	Yes	Teletype ASR 33
	Other	Pushbuttons, Teletypewriter	Thumbwheel switches	Computer	—
OUTPUT	**Mediums**				
	Magnetic Tape	Yes	Yes	Yes	No
	Paper Tape	Yes	Yes	No	Yes
	Punched Cards	Yes	No	No	No
	On-Line	Yes (see Comments)	Yes	Yes	No
	Other	No	No	—	Teletypewriter
	Format Control Patch Panel	No	No	No	Yes
	Other	Software	Software	Software	Software (see Comments)

CHARACTERISTICS	Max Speed, inches/sec	12-20	30	5	Operator limited
	Resolution, inches	0.001	0.005	0.001	0.001 (or 0.02mm)
	Accuracy, inches	±0.01	±0.005	±0.003	±0.005
	Digitizing Modes	Incremental, absolute	Point; line	Manual	—
	Scaling	Yes (with computer)	Yes	Yes	Yes (see Comments)
	Grid Roundoff	Yes (with computer)	Yes	Yes	Yes (see Comments)
	Other	—	—	—	—
MINIMUM PRICE, $		6,000 (OEM price)	40,000	80,000	25,500
COMMENTS		When used on-line, system is effectively a man-machine interface	Film projection also available		First output tape from teletypewriter punch First tape can be run through external PDP 8/L for processing; second tape, from supplied high-speed punch, reformatted for application; has scaling and grid roundoff corrections Intended primarily for IC mask making Table tilts; nixie tube display of position Software for PDP 8/L

N/A - Not Applicable

• Optional

IDENTITY		Unitech Programming System 28	University Computing LARR-M	University Computing LARR-V	University Computing Oscar F Digitizing System
REPORT NUMBER					
TYPE		Electromechanical (drafting table)	Electromechanical (drafting table)	Electromechanical (drafting table)	Semiautomatic strip-chart
USABLE DIGITIZING AREA, inches		42 x 60	48 x 60	48 x 60	13 x 26
INPUT	**Cursor**	Yes (armless)	Yes	Yes	Yes
	Keyboard	Teletype ASR 33	Yes	Yes	Yes
	Other		Stylus	Stylus	Function keys
OUTPUT	**Mediums**				
	Magnetic Tape	No	Yes	No	No
	Paper Tape	Yes	No	Yes*	Yes*
	Punched Cards	No	No	Yes	Yes
	On-Line	No (see Comments)	No	No	No
	Other	Teletypewriter	Teletypewriter*	No	No
	Format Control Patch Panel	No	Yes	Yes	Yes
	Other	Software	No	No	Teletypewriter

CHARACTERISTICS	Max Speed, inches/sec	Operator limited	Operator limited	Operator limited	Operator limited
	Resolution, inches	0.001 (or 0.02mm)	250, 500, 1,000 counts/inch (see Comments)	250, 500, 1,000 or 100, 200, 400 counts/inch	0.010
	Accuracy, inches	±0.005	±0.008	±0.008	1% of full scale of each channel
	Digitizing Modes	—	Absolute (see Comments)	Absolute	Absolute
	Scaling	Yes	Yes*	Yes*	No
	Grid Roundoff	Yes	Yes*	Yes*	No
	Other	—	—	—	—
MINIMUM PRICE, $		33,500 (with PDP 8/E) 35,500 (with PDP 8/L)	28,600	16,500	8,950
COMMENTS		Intended primarily for IC mask making System includes int. control processor — PDP 8/E or PDP 8/L System includes high-speed paper tape punch Software puts output tape in proper format for intended application Int. processor can be used as independent computer Table tilts; nixie tube display of position	Screen can be back-lighted* Manufacturer gives resolution in counts/inch; can also be 100, 200, and 400 counts/inch for this system Incremental operation possible*	Screen can be back-lighted*	Backlighted viewing screen Film projector for 16mm, 35mm, and 70mm film* Accepts roll paper up to 12.5" wide, rolls up to 5" in diameter

N/A - Not Applicable

* Optional

IDENTITY		University Computing Oscar K Digitizing System	University Computing Oscar S Digitizing System	Graph-Data Digitizing DATATRACE DI-1400	Graph-Data Digitizing DATATRACE DI-1500
REPORT NUMBER				–	–
TYPE		Stripchart	Electromechanical (drum)	Electromechanical	Electromechanical and electrooptical
USABLE DIGITIZING AREA, inches		13 x 25 (viewing) 12 x 16 (reading)	20 x 20	9.00 x 36.00	9.00 x 36.00
INPUT	Cursor	Yes	Yes	No	No
	Keyboard	Yes	Yes	No	No
	Other	Function keys	Function keys	Tracing stylus	Automatic optical line follower
OUTPUT	Mediums Magnetic Tape	No	Yes*	No	No
	Paper Tape	Yes*	Yes*	Yes	Yes
	Punched Cards	Yes	Yes	No	No
	On-Line	No	No	No	No
	Other	Teletypewriter	Teletypewriter	TTW telephone coupling*	TTW telephone coupling*
	Format Control Patch Panel	Yes	Yes	Yes*	Yes*
	Other	No	No	Tape-to-card software is provided	Tape-to-card software is provided

CHARACTERISTICS	Max Speed, inches/sec	Operator limited	50	10	0.2
	Resolution, inches	0.010	1,000 counts/inch	0.009	0.009
	Accuracy, inches	1% of full scale of each trace	±0.004	0.01	0.01
	Digitizing Modes	Absolute	Absolute	Point (absolute)	Automatic (absolute)
	Scaling	No	No	No	No
	Grid Roundoff	No	No	No	No
	Other	No	No	Adaptable to very long records	Adaptable to very long records
MINIMUM PRICE, $		7,050	25,400	5,000 (price includes Friden SP2 Punch)	15,000 (price includes Friden SP2 Punch)
COMMENTS		Backlighted viewing screen Accepts roll paper up to 12.5" wide, rolls up to 5" in diameter	Backlighted viewing screen Film projector for 16mm, 35mm, and 70mm film* Accepts roll paper up to 20" wide, rolls up to 5" in diameter	Over 600 points per hour can be digitized. Tape-reading program for IBM 360/30 including line-printer replotting option is included; software for 1108 computer is in preparation.	Sampling (digitizing) options include automatic peak detection. Tape reading program availability same as for DI-1400 Digitizer.

N/A - Not Applicable

*** Optional**

IDENTITY		Data Tech MSD–30	Gerber OLF–1	Bendix Graphscan	
REPORT NUMBER		41.030.02	41.047.03	—	
TYPE		Electromechanical	Line following	All electronic	
USABLE DIGITIZING AREA, inches		See Comments	60 x 96 to 60 x 288	17 x 17; 22 x 34; 34 x 44; 40 x 60	
INPUT	**Cursor**	No	See Comments	Yes	
	Keyboard	No	Yes	No	
	Other	Encoders	Switches; controls	No	
OUTPUT	**Mediums**				
	Magnetic Tape	Yes*	Yes	No	
	Paper Tape	Yes*	Yes	Yes	
	Punched Cards	Yes	No	Yes	
	On-Line	Yes*	No	Yes	
	Other	Printer*	—	Teletype	
	Format Control Patch Panel	Yes	No	No	
	Other	—	—	—	

CHARACTERISTICS	Max Speed, inches/sec	—	180	300	
	Resolution, inches	See Comments	0.010	0.010	
	Accuracy, inches	See Comments	0.003	0.010	
	Digitizing Modes	Point	Automatic; manual; semiautomatic	Absolute	
	Scaling	No	Yes	No	
	Grid Roundoff	No	No	No	
	Other	—	—	—	
MINIMUM PRICE, $		From manufacturer	200,000 (approx)	7,150	
COMMENTS		System consists of encoders and console; encoders with resolution from 10 to 2,500 lines per revolution available	Head follows line automatically; manual control possible		

• Optional

GLOSSARY

Analog. Pertains to data represented in the form of continuously variable physical quantities (e.g., voltage or angular position). Contrast with *digital.*

Automatic Drafting Machine. A large flatbed digital plotter.

Baud. A unit of signaling speed equal to the number of discrete conditions or signal events per second. *Note*: In the case of a train of binary signals, and therefore in most data communications applications, one baud equals one bit per second.

Comparator Chart. A precise photographic image of an engineering component, projected for comparison and reference during the machining of the part.

Computer. A device capable of solving problems by accepting data, performing prescribed operations on the data, and supplying the results of these operations—all without intervention by a human operator.

Data Processing. A systematic sequence of operations performed upon data, e.g., handling, computing, merging, sorting, or any other transformation or rearrangement in which the object is to extract information, revise the data, or alter its representation.

Data Set. A device that serves as modulator and/or demodulator. Synonymous with *modem.* Provides the appropriate interface between a communications link and a data processing machine or system.

Digital. Pertains to data represented in the form of digits. Contrast with *analog.*

Digital-to-Analog Converter. A device that converts the representation of data from digital to analog form.

Digital Plotter. A device that moves a pen, a stylus, a spot of light, or other implement over a surface under digital control to produce hard-copy output.

Digitize. To change analog quantities to digital form.

Digitizer. A device that converts to digital form the shape of the path followed by some kind of sensor.

Drum Plotter. A digital plotter in which the plot is produced by the combined movements of a pen carriage across the plot and the rotation of a drum bearing the paper on which the plot is being generated.

Drum-Type Plotter. A digital plotter in which the plot is generated by the combined movements of pen and paper, as in a drum plotter.

Flow Chart. A diagram that shows the structure and general sequence of operations of a program or process by means of symbols and interconnecting lines which represent operations, data, flow, and equipment.

Fatbed Digitizer. A digitizer with its own dedicated, flat working surface.

Flatbed Plotter. A digital plotter in which the plotting medium is held on a dedicated, flat working surface.

FORTRAN *(FORmula TRANslating System).* High-level programming language intended for scientific and engineering application.

Hardware. Physical equipment, such as mechanical, magnetic, electrical, and electronic devices. Contrast with *software.*

Hardwired. A hardwired controller or computer is one in which the program is determined by the constructions of the device, i.e., the program cannot be varied.

Image Digitizer. See *Digitizer.*

Incremental. Step by step, discontinuous. An incremental motion is one that takes place in a series of steps, the mechanism coming to rest at the end of each step.

Interpolation. In digital plotting and numerically controlled machine-tool usage, refers to the capability of a system to generate a line or curve in response to a single command, the sequence of steps necessary to attain this result being generated internally.

Line Printer. Prints all characters that comprise one line during each cycle of its action. Synonymous with "line-at-a-time printer." *Note*: Two widely used types of line printers are chain printers and drum printers.

Modem (Data Set). A modem (modulator-demodulator) or data set is a device that provides the appropriate interface between a data processing machine and a communications line. Converts data originating in digital form into analog signals suitable for transmission over telephone lines (and vice versa).

Mylar. A drafting medium with high dimensional stability.

Nixie Tube. A type of neon tube that displays one of a fixed set of characters, typically the digits 0 through 9.

Nonimpact Printer. A printer using any printing technique other than the physical impact of an inked character form against the paper.

Off-Line. Pertains to equipment or devices that are not in direct communications with the central processor of a computer system. Contrast with *on-line. Note*: Off-line devices cannot be controlled by a computer except through human intervention.

On-Line. Pertains to equipment or devices in direct communication with the central processor of a computer system. Contrast with *off-line. Note*: On-line devices are usually under the direct control of the computer with which they are in communication.

Operations Research. The use of analytical techniques to solve operational problems in order to provide management with a sound, logical basis for making decisions and predictions. Among the common techniques of operation research are linear programming, Monte Carlo methods, information theory, and queueing theory.

Peel Coat. A laminated mylar photographic-plotting medium. Plotting on peel coat involves removal of an upper layer to expose a sensitized base.

PERT. Program evaluation and review technique. A planning and scheduling method in which the activities involved in a project are represented as a connected network.

Program. (1)A plan for solving a problem. (2) To devise a plan for solving a problem. (3) A computer routine, i.e., a set of instructions arranged in proper sequence to cause a computer to perform a particular process. (4) To write a computer routine.

Programmer. A person who devises programs. *Note*: The term "programmer" is most suitably applied to a person who is mainly involved in formulating programs, particularly at the level of flow chart preparation. A person concerned with the definition of problems is called an analyst, while a person who converts programs into coding suitable for entry into a computer system is called a coder. In many organizations, all three of these functions are performed by "programmers."

Programming Language. An unambiguous language used to express programs for a computer.

Sawyer Principle. A proprietary drive system used in digital plotters manufactured by Xynetics Inc., in which the plotting motion is generated by the interaction of electromagnets in the plotting head with a fixed waffle pattern of magnetic material.

Software. The collection of programs and routines associated with a computer (such as assemblers, compilers, utility routines, and operating systems) which facilitate the programming and operation of the computer. Contrast with *hardware.*

Sprocket Holes. Holes punched in a paper tape or in one or both longitudinal margins of a continuous form to facilitate feeding of the tape or form.

Storage Tube. A type of cathode-ray tube in which the image is stored on the screen of the tube, allowing continuous display without constant regeneration.

Teletypewriter. Trade name used by AT&T to refer to telegraph-terminal equipment.

Time Sharing. (1) The use of a given device by a number of other devices, programs, or human users, one at a time and in rapid succession. (2) A technique or system for furnishing computing services to multiple users simultaneously, providing rapid responses to each of them. *Note*: Time-sharing computer systems usually employ multiprogramming and/or multiprocessing techniques, and they are often capable of serving users at remote locations via a data communications network.

Vellum. A heavy paper used in drafting.

INDEX